100 Days in The Ghan

By: Tom A. Wiggins

U.S. Army Airborne Ranger (Retired)

Rated **R** for Ranger Content

READER DISCRETION ADVISED

100 Days in The Ghan

First Edition

Library of Congress Cataloging-in-Publication Data
Library of Congress Catalog Card Number:

Wiggins, Thomas A.
    100 Days in The Ghan / Thomas A. Wiggins
    p. cm.
    ISBN # 978-0-615-16623-0
    I. Title

First Edition, First Printing, softcover, October 2007. Edited by Mike Blackwell, Print Northwest, McMinnville, Oregon. Published by Thomas A. Wiggins. Printed by Oregon Lithoprint, McMinnville, Oregon.

Printed in the U.S.A.

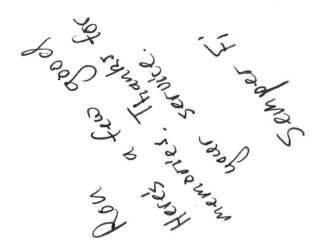

> "I ain't too good with words and whatnot, but I think I tell a damn good story."

Ranger Wiggins

Table of Contents

Preface

In the words of Gunny Brandon, the following is a "mostly true story." I'm not a writer just someone with an extraordinary story who refused to have some "ghostwriter" try to tell you about something he didn't experience. Some names were changed so that I hopefully won't get sued. My readers also must realize that much of what the Rangers do remains classified for a very long time, therefore, there are many missions I could not include in the book, but I feel there is more than enough to keep your attention. I tried to stay as true to what has happened as I can remember but let's face it: I got shot in the head so it probably isn't perfect. I don't have much of an imagination so enjoy the pictures. Rangers aren't allowed to take cameras, so I don't really have many pictures from the first couple of deployments, but later after I had been around a while I learned ways around all of that and I took some pretty good ones. That being said, I am not hoping for a best seller I just wanted our story put on paper so that hopefully none of us will ever forget what we accomplished. I hope that you enjoy!

Dedications

This Book is Dedicated to:

Ranger Art Sellers
Ranger Mark Hurst
Ranger Sean Jaeger
Ranger Toney Kvam

and

All of the brave warriors of
Aco. 1/75th Ranger Regiment.

Rangers Lead the Way!!!

9/11

"Aw man! I told you the movie doesn't start till 7! Now what are we goin' to do for the next hour and a half?!"

"We could go bum around Wal-Mart," Lance suggested.

"Hey yeah my year probation is up! I'm allowed to go in Wal-Mart now," John exclaimed, "We should go let them know." Yup, we were the typical group of freshman hooligans. Our first year of freedom, experience, and life in the real world. Just a year ago John had been arrested for petty theft when caught stealing a twenty cent fishing hook from Wal-Mart! The funny part is he wound up paying $200 for it and was banned from Wal-Mart for one year. Now I despise liars and thieves but John; John was just fun!

As we slowly trudged around the corner to the store we cracked jokes at each other's expense and Josh, being the biggest of us all at the time, was doing his best to let us know. As we entered Wal-Mart we were greeted by an elderly gentleman with a spry "welcome to Wal-Mart."

I said "Yeah it's been a while for some of us," laughing at my own stupid joke. We all took turn shaking the greeter's hand which we all found humorous, but in all honesty I had always loved the old man.

John seemed to be lost in old memories as we ventured farther into the store playing with everything not tied down. A couple of weeks before, we had discovered the Razor scooters were up for grabs and got in trouble for racing through the store on them. They're tied down now. As

Lance, Josh, and I were checking out the lingerie I looked around for John to make sure he was keeping his hands in his pockets as agreed upon before entering the store.

"Oh shit guys where's John?"

"Probably in the discount section," Josh suggested.

"Yeah the five finger discount section," Lance barely got out before roaring with laughter. "We better find him quick!"

It didn't take long to locate John. He was still at the entrance of the store talking to recruiters for the U.S. Army. "Oh my God what in the hell is John doing now?" The four of us had on many occasions been reprimanded in high school for messing with recruiters. One time especially was pretty serious; we had "hid" a recruiter's laptop that he had on his display table. It was his own fault though he was off flirting with some girls when he should have been with his gear! I told the guys to wait while I went to go get John.

As I came up on the recruiters I began apologizing to them saying "come on John, I'm sorry he's just been so excited since you guys started letting gays in the military." I managed to tear John away from his little friends and as we were catching up with the rest of the guys, I asked John what he was saying to the recruiters. "No man I wasn't messing with them I think it would be cool to be an M.P." John told me.

"What in the hell is a M.P." I asked.

"Come on man Military Police, don't you know anything about the Army?" John asked shocked.

"Dude ok I have a theory on the Army. The Army is made up 99% of wimps from high school who feel they have something to prove, .5% of people who just see it as the only way to get out of their shitty town, and .5% badasses." John laughed "agreed."

We finally found the rest of the guys back at the theater playing video games in the lobby. "Thanks for waiting guys!"

"Well you looked like you two were getting lovey dovey with the recruiters so we bailed!" Lance laughed. We saw the last movie together before our entire world and lives changed that night. *How High,* I must say it was funny but a little too ghetto for my taste.

I woke up the next morning at 5 a.m. which was the norm because Josh and I were masons and we had to be to work at 6 a.m. We usually got home around 4 or 4:30 p.m. which gave us just enough time to both get showered and make it to school on time. I usually got home from school around 10:30 p.m. to find John and Lance having some sort of party. By this time at night I was dead tired but still had to study... and maybe party a little bit! This usually found me getting in bed around 2:30 a.m. then up again at 5 a.m. to do it all over again. This was killing me! About once every 2 weeks I couldn't even get up to go to work and I'd just sleep all day. I think my bosses understood because anyone else would have been fired if they tried to pull that mess.

Today we were building apartments in northwest Gainesville. It was all work and rarely talk on the jobsite. An occasional joke here and there but mostly just "gettin with it," always rushing. Today was no different. That is until about 10 a.m. when my boss, Scooter, showed up.

"Hey Scooter what's up?" I asked not really caring.

"Have you heard on the radio?" he asked.

"Heard what? Is it going to storm today?"

"Hell no Tom someone has flown two airplanes into the World Trade Center in New York City," Scooter says. "What?!" I questioned in surprise. "Yeah, evidently they are expecting a lot of casualties".

"Wait...so was it an accident?"

"Well they haven't said yet, but I don't see how two planes accidentally fly into the WTC in 5 minutes."

"You're right, let's turn on the radio I wanna hear this. It sounds crazy!" And sure enough there it was all over the radio. I was shocked, but none of the laborers seemed bothered by it. After listening for a while another plane that was headed for the Pentagon went down in Pennsylvania. For me this was getting out of control. How long would this last? How many more planes would be hijacked? How many more innocent people would die? Almost everyone I worked with was pretty much uneducated and no one could seem to understand what all of this would mean. But I knew. I knew someone was going to have to pay for the thousands of lives that were taken that day. The rest of my crew felt bad for the people who died but thought my claim that there would be a war because of it seemed ridiculous.

When I got home that evening the events of what had now been dubbed 9/11 were all over the T.V. and of course would be replayed for weeks, months, and even years. But this was the first time I had seen the planes actually hitting the buildings, the buildings collapsing, and people trying to escape. As my roommates and I sat there watching, we were all pretty silent. No one made a crack. School had been cancelled for the day because of the attacks so we just sat there all night watching everything unfold. We saw families crying for their lost ones and people from Pakistan partying and burning American flags in the street. All of this caused a spark in my group of friends. None of us liked it but what could we do?

Sleeping giant awakened!

In the days following 9/11 President Bush would make a speech saying that the American government knew who was behind the attacks and they would pay for their actions. He said "we will not falter we will not fail" and "if you are not with us then you are against us."

All of the sudden there was no more partying in the streets of Pakistan no more flag burning. The world knew we were serious.

Later that day I was driving by the main entrance of the University of Florida and I couldn't believe what I saw. A group of college students were having a 72 hour vigil for peace. They had signs saying "no eye for an eye" and "Timothy McViegh is a terrorist too."

This was too much for me to handle. I'm all about freedom of speech, but it's beyond me how anyone can think like this. Yeah Timothy McViegh was a terrorist and he got what was coming to him too!

That evening when we got home, Lance and I told Josh and John about the 72 hour vigil for peace. After awhile of bitching about it, we decided to do something. I had a flag that said "Kill them all let God sort them out." (At the time little did I know it was actually a Ranger flag.) We also took an American flag and went down to the corner where we saw the people that day. We set up shop on the corner across from them. Within two hours hundreds of people who had driven by and seen us were on our side of the road holding everything from flags to homemade poster boards. We stayed out there all week. We didn't go to work, we didn't go to school ...we all felt that this was bigger than any of that.

Pictures from Post 9/11 Rally

As the week progressed the rally started to get a lot of media attention from the local T.V. stations and such. As Lance and I were the ones to start the entire thing, we were asked to give a short interview explaining why we were there. During this interview we were asked, "So if you were called up to go fight in the war on terrorism, would you?" Of course we both very passionately informed the media that yes, we would.

When the rally was over and we were all at home, we talked about the possibility of joining the military. Suddenly for the first time in any of our lives, it seemed like a really great idea. The next question was which branch we would join. We all quickly agreed that it couldn't be Air Force or Navy. So we had come to the conclusion it would either have to be Marines or Army. My sister had recently graduated high school and enlisted in the Marines, and I knew from the get go I would have to outdo her. So it was decided...we wanted to be Special Operations. After much discussion we decided none of us liked the water enough to be SEALS, but we all liked the idea of jumping out of airplanes, especially the thought of getting paid to jump out of airplanes. Oh how little did we know! So we all decided with the exception of John, who still wanted to be a M.P. We wanted to be Airborne Rangers!

The very next week we wandered into the Army recruiting station.

"Oh my God what in the hell do you guys want?!" screamed Sgt. Brown. Oh yes, as I thought they all remembered us. This should be fun.

"Hey man we want to join the Army," Lance told him.

"Yeah right you punks just want to waste our time we got better things to do," said the sergeant still using his outside voice.

"Hey no man we aren't kidding. We wanna go get a little revenge. We figure the quickest way to get to the war is to be an Airborne Ranger so where do I sign?"

"Ah well if you were serious you would want to talk to Sgt. Lopez. He's a Ranger," Brown told us "But he isn't here right now."

"Well damn, who do we talk to?" Josh asked. The recruiter was still skeptical but he showed us into the station commander's office as he couldn't pass up on a chance to fill the monthly quota in a single day.

We all sat with the station commander for a while asking questions and telling him what we wanted. He told us some of what he knew about the Rangers, which wasn't much, and told us how difficult Ranger training was and that the odds of all four of us making it through were very slim. During this time SSG Lopez, the Ranger, came in. He was walking by the office when the commander yelled, "Hey Lopez, these guys wanna be Rangers." SSG Lopez stuck his head in the door, looked at us and yelled, "these guys don't wanna be Rangers!" and slammed the door and marched off. At first I assumed that we had a previous encounter with this SSG. Lopez, but as we soon figured out all the tough screaming was just a show!

As the next month progressed, the four of us went through a lot of trials with our parents. None of our parents or guardians was happy at all about our new strong desire to enlist in the military. The first of the "fearless four" to back out was John. John simply had a horrible commitment problem and had no urge to leave his home for God knows how long. The next to fall was Lance. Lance had always been somewhat of a momma's boy; not because he wanted to, but because his mom made sure he was. He could never escape her no matter where he was or what he was doing. When she found out what we were planning, she went nuts. For some reason she blamed it all on me and thought that I had "put all of these crazy ideas into his head". It was really the other way around. Lance was the only one of us who had any knowledge of what exactly an Airborne Ranger was. So after many fights and threats, Lance gave into his mom and aborted the pact we had all made. However, the next semester Lance joined the ROTC at the University of Florida.

Now there were only two of us left: Josh and I the dynamic duo! While the recruiters were getting our paperwork squared away, Josh and I decided we should probably take some initiative to start getting into shape for the army. We were already in pretty decent shape from working construction. We started getting up even earlier for our long day to run a few miles each morning; this wasn't as bad as it sounds as we had both dropped out of school at this point. Anytime we had a free moment we were training. Our last couple of weeks as a civilian we even quit our jobs and spent a great deal of time preparing ourselves. One day we road marched from Hawthorne to Gainesville and back, which is a little over 19 miles each way. Not knowing any better we did this in the day time IN FLORIDA and I wore Sketchers. We filled make shift rucksacks with dumbbells from home and when it was all said and done we probably had about 90 pounds worth of gear on each of us. When bragging to my great uncle who had been in the Army his entire life about what Josh and I had done, he told me, "Better at least double up on the weight next time if you wanna be a Ranger!" All of this crazy talk had me a bit worried, so we trained even harder.

During this time Josh and I had also been building what we called "The Green Mile." It was an obstacle course in the woods behind my house that definitely seemed a mile. We stretched barbed wire over the creek to low crawl under, built a 30ft. wall to climb, installed pull-up stations, and much more. We even had plans to install a zip-line, but our funding was limited as we had both quit our jobs. Either way we felt our obstacle course was intense and put it to the test while my sister was at home.

Misty had not long ago finished Marine boot camp and we figured Marine boot camp and Army basic training couldn't be that different. With this in mind, we had Misty try out our obstacle course. Misty had always been a runner and did a good job on our course as a lot of it was running. She even knocked out the pull-ups, which kind of embarrassed me at the time because that was my weak point. The only difficulty she had was getting up the 30ft. wall. She just couldn't make it. "Your rope is too skinny!" Misty fired back at our hysterical laughter. "And there is no way you will ever have to climb a wall this high" her defensiveness grew as we assured her that we had been doing it every day! But Misty was of great help that day. She informed us that we should work mostly on our pull-ups because we would have to "knock out" ten before each meal, and if we couldn't do the required ten, we would be sent to the back of the line each time. This scared the shit out of Josh and me because if you know us we are definitely eaters!

Finally D-Day was insight. "Alright fags you guys will have to go back to MEPS (Military Entrance Processing Station) to ship out" SSG Lopez informed Josh and I as we high fived. We already had an experience at the MEPS when we had to go get physicals and do our paperwork, and needless to say it was a blast. Not the actual process but the nights that you have to spend in a hotel with hundreds of horny teenagers getting ready to ship off with nothing but a guarantee of no sex for a few months at the minimum. I could spare you the details but I'm not the type. One of the young ladies that I had "encounters" with was a cute little 18 year old redhead who was getting ready to ship out to the Navy the next day. She swore up and down to me that she was a virgin and she wanted to lose her virginity before she got on a boat with a bunch of horny squids. I didn't question it! We "trained" about five times that night, which had Josh pissed off because he was my roommate and every time we did it she wanted him to leave the room.

So we were at MEPS getting through all of the red tape, i.e. physicals, contracts, and swearing the oath. Now getting Ranger training in your contract is a mission in itself. The Army doesn't like to guarantee such specialized training because it cost lots of money to train a soldier, and if something goes wrong and a person cant make it to Ranger training they can scream breach of contract and get out of the Army. The Army personnel who were drawing up my contract kept feeding me bullshit about how there were no Ranger training slots. Ranger Lopez had already talked to me about this. He just said not to give up and tell them maybe you will come back another time when they do have a slot for Ranger training. Eventually I got what I wanted, but I had to compromise. The Army gave me a Ranger training slot for going through Nuclear Biological Chemical (NBC) School. Sounds high speed right … I didn't know better. Though we originally wanted to go in on the buddy plan so we could be stationed together, Josh decided not to hold out for the Ranger slot so he became Infantry with Airborne in his contract, mainly for the $20,000 signing bonus. So off we went Josh headed for Ft. Benning, Georgia and I headed for Ft. Lenordwood, Missouri.

Oh by the way a tip for all you would-be recruits … remember when filling out the medical section of your enlistment papers NO stands for Numerous Opportunities and YES stands for Your Enlistment Stops. If you say that YES that you have some sort of medical condition, you're probably going home. Strangely enough I had several but managed to slip through the cracks by simply not admitting them. I had grown up with asthma, had several surgeries for ear infections, and have abnormally large balls. The doctor giving me my physical for sure saw two of my problems but decided to ignore them thank God.

Basic Depression

I personally had so much fun in basic training it was ridiculous, but everyone else was very depressed. I got it in my head before I even boarded the plane that I was in for some shit. I was imagining *Full Metal Jacket,* getting our ass beat every day and shit like that. The first shock came my first minute there. I was with girls! As it turns out basic training and Nuclear Biological Chemical (NBC) School were combined here. The first half consisted of learning your basic skills i.e. physical training (PT), marksmanship and such and the second half learning how to recon and decon an NBC attack. I immediately thought to myself, great, this is going to be gay. It became evident immediately that there was going to be special treatment. The girls didn't have to shave their heads ... hell some of them needed to shave their face worse than me! PT scoring was different between the girls and guys too, I could go all day, but there is no point. The fact is that if the U.S. military did not have women in the force we would probably be a Republic of China or some shit.

I found out quickly that all of the PT I did as a civilian would be useless. The first two weeks of basic training are used to break the body down so that the Army can rebuild you the way they want. The phrases I will never forget are, "attention to detail, team works the key," and "hurry up waiting on you!" Every time we were not in perfect order (which is every two minutes) we had to get in the front lean and rest position (push up) and on the way down yell "attention to detail" on the way up "team work's the key". I learned fast that it was the best to be last into the chow hall because everyone got about the same amount of time to eat (two minutes), and if you were the first out the drill sergeants make you do some sort of exercise while waiting for the rest of your comrades which really sucks right after eating.

When you get to basic you are assigned a battle buddy and you two are responsible for each other. So in other words if your battle buddy screws up, you are both held responsible. My luck I had a thug from the Bronx for my first battle buddy. Pvt. Johnson was his name but as you will see I had an array of special titles for him.

On the second day he got into a fight with our drill sergeant and we were kicked out of the platoon with no guidance. We had to pack up all of our gear into duffle bags and carry them around and ask other platoons if we could join them. This was what is known in the Army as a typical fuck fuck game. Of course none of the other platoons wanted the "troublemakers" of the company. But then something unexpected happened.

A New Home

"Hey dawg, fuck this, lets just start our own platoon," said 2pac (Pvt. Johnson). By this time I was so pissed with this guy he was damn lucky that they hadn't issued us weapons yet!

"Yeah that's a great idea that's almost as good as the one you had that I should carry your bag for you … you're a fucking moron!"

"Man why you gotta be like that I aint never done nuttin to you," retaliated private shit for brains.

"Are you out of your mind, I've been getting yelled at and smoked to death because of you since I got here!"

"Man fuck you I'm goin' to ask the D.I. if we can start our own platoon!" shouted the kid with a strong Jamaican accent.

"Hey man here's your fair warning if I have to do one more push up because of you its not gonna be good for you." "Whateva" is all I got as he trailed off for the D.I. (drill instructor) office.

"What the fuck do you want now Johnson, still looking for a home?!" screamed the Drill Sergeant.

Standing at parade rest "Drill Sergeant, Private Johnson and Private Wiggins could not find a home and wish to form our own platoon Drill Sergeant."

"What the fuck? Wiggins was this your idea? This shit for brains didn't think of this on his own!"

"Negative drill sergeant it was Johnson's idea but unless you let us back in we have no other choice."

"And what the hell are you going to call your

platoon Pri (slang for private)? Who's going to train you? Two people barely make up a fire team!" he continued to barrage us with questions.

"Our platoon name could be Killerz." I stupidly chimed in and without following up with a "Drill Sergeant". While doing the 25 push ups for not remembering to end a sentence with drill sergeant the D.I. yelled at me, "so you to think you are killers huh?"

"Drill Sergeant, Johnson probably is and at this rate I will be soon!" Again not the answer he was looking for more push ups!

"You know what Pri's I think this is a lovely idea this way we can get rid of all of the other losers and dump them into your platoon" yelled the drill sergeant delightfully. "Johnson go wait in the hall close the door behind you, Wiggins get up you stay" the drill sergeant instructed and as Johnson left I got to parade rest. The Drill Sergeant at that point relieved all of my fears telling me that he knew I was squared away and Johnson was the piece of shit and not to lose motivation. And so 5th platoon was formed. We still slept, trained, and ate with our old platoon, 4th platoon, but we formed up as 5th platoon separately. Private Johnson only lasted about a week before he punched another Drill Sergeant and got kicked out of the Army, but by this point there were about 10 Killerz.

My new battle buddy had just got kicked out of his platoon was exactly the opposite of Johnson. He was a complete pussy but what always got him into trouble was that he questioned every single thing that we did. He was one of those guys who always had a "better" way to do everything ... which doesn't work in the army. At either rate I would be stuck with him for the rest of basic training and AIT (Advanced Individual Training), however, he wound up not graduating and therefore it was all for nothing.

We were on our final FTX (field training excerise) of basic training and my battle buddy decided to catch a little shut eye during an exercise and got busted. The results were that both of us got to pull three hours of guard a night for the remainder of the exercise! I was so pissed off we barely got any sleep as it was and this would leave us with about two hours of sleep. Not to mention is was a whopping ten degrees outside! I remember waking up one morning and my feet were outside of our little tent and had about a foot of snow on them (Little did I know I would have much more experience with snow).

My Basic Training Class

My First "Kill"

I had many proud moments in basic training weather it was at the range or in the classroom but this one was the best. This event took place during the final FTX as well. Platoon Killerz were the enemy and the Bulldawgs were gonna be looking for us. Killerz was the smallest of all of the platoons and the hardest to control (mostly shitbags). So our plan was that there was no plan everyone took off everyman for himself. My battle buddy for once decided he wanted to stick with me. We were standing in a valley bullshittin' when we heard voices.

"Holy shit man is that them already? Why in the hell are they being so loud?"

"Quick hide!" spouted off my battle buddy, but I was already moving. As I dove behind a couple of fallen trees I looked back and saw my battle buddy's idea of hiding. He was standing behind the tree that we were talking at peeking around to see what he could. Oh my God I thought, this guy will never make it. I wanted to yell for him too move but it was to late. I started to question my own cover and concealment.

So here they came. I couldn't help but laugh. If I had a couple of grenades I could have finished the entire group in a matter of seconds. Just as they were coming around my battle buddy's tree, I decided, oh well it's too late for him and rang out the first shot. He was immediately killed, but when the "enemy" fire continued there was a huge sense of confusion. The Bulldawgs Drill Sergeant was yelling at them, "you're under attack do something"! They began running around with their heads up their asses as I continued to pick them off one by one. When that last SIM (Simulation round that lights up vest when person is shot) round was fired and that last vest lit up I could hear the Drill Sergeant ask my comrade "who was with you?" My battle buddy told him with a little smile and drill sergeant Colon hollered, "ok you won Ranger Wiggins come out." I questioned it. Could this be a trick? I just laid there while he called out for me. Little did anyone realize that I was a mere fifteen meters in front of them. They had been looking at me the entire time and never saw me. I waited for the platoon to leave before I ever came out. My battle buddy was hysterical.

The next day I bumped into D.I. Colon. By this point I had somewhat proven myself in that the entire basic training staff learned that I had Ranger training in my contract so I was forced to do everything ten times better than everyone else i.e. if the company ran two miles I was running six.

"Hey Drill Sergeant, how are your boys?" I asked grinning ear to ear.

"Yeah yeah, good job yesterday Wiggins, but I wonder if you'd still be smiling today if your battle buddy had really been killed?" asked Colon killing the mood.

Being the complete smartass I am "Probably feel a lot better than if I had gotten my whole platoon killed!" And just like that I screwed my battle buddy for the first time. My comment landed us on brass detail which meant we had to try to collect five thousand bullet casings, which at the moment didn't seem bad because the exercise had lasted over a week and I was sure that there were over one-hundred thousand rounds lying about, plus everyone was picking up brass. The catch was if we didn't find five thousand pieces of brass we had to do a push up for every piece that we were missing. With time winding down the task seemed impossible, and we started begging others for the brass that they had collected. When time was up, we were still easily short fifteen hundred casings as we trudged over to the Drill Sergeant.

"Here ya go Drill Sergeant five-thousand two hundred and eighty-seven casings," I flat out lied praying to God he would not make us count them for him.

Colon just rolled his eyes "Alright set them there and go." Figures, I thought, just another typical Army fuck fuck game, but for once I was happy.

As I said earlier, in my Army career I would have many more experiences with snow, but my experiences at Ft. Leanordwood I will always remember best I think because they were my first. One morning 0430 hours in our PT's (physical training uniforms) ready for some physical training, it was announced that there would be no training that day due to snow. At first I thought it was a joke I mean even if we couldn't train outside I was certain they would have classroom stuff for us to do. As it turned at it had snowed so much that night that hardly anyone could get out of their driveway, so we had one Drill Sergeant who had to manage approximately 200 privates. We were instructed to clean the barracks and our gear which was stupid as everything was already spotless as that is how it was always required to be. My buddies and I saw this as a perfect opportunity to get caught up on some much deserved sleep (which was, of course, forbidden). The three of us were racked out in the laundry room which seemed like the perfect plan, but of course it was destined to fail. Sure enough we were caught before noon and detailed to shoveling snow off of all of the sidewalks. I remember thinking to myself this isn't so bad, I've never shoveled snow before. Then it hit me ... I had never thrown a snowball before! I couldn't resist. And as I released, he appeared out of the corner of my eye. Where in the hell did he come from I had just made a sweep before I threw and saw no one!

"Wiggins!!!!" screamed the Drill sergeant at the top of his lungs "What in the hell are you doing? You are just having too much fun aren't you? Well that's ok I have another assignment for you since you like playing in the snow so much. You and your two sleeping beauties over there need to build snow forts all the way around the barracks to make sure that we are secure tonight."

"Sweet! Roger that Drill Sergeant" I spouted off without thinking as usual. The Drill Sergeant just shook his head and shuffled back inside. I think it was to cold for him to waste anymore time on me; it was hella cold!

What seemed so cool at first was quickly becoming a nightmare. We had already been outside for a little over three hours and had only built two forts. It was easily in the negative temperatures, though I can't remember exactly how cold it was but the wind was whippin'! It wasn't just the cold that was uncomfortable, we were now soaked pretty much from head to toe. Finally the company started forming up for dinner chow and we were called to fall in. After enduring another hour of being wet and freezing, we returned back to the warm barracks. I immediately changed into dry fatigues, but it was too late, something bad was happening. No matter what I did I couldn't get warm. I had virtually every issued item of clothing on wrapped myself in blankets but nothing helped I couldn't get warm thank goodness lights out was only an hour away and I didn't have fire guard tonight.

0430 hours time to get ready for PT still feeling like shit. I take a piss and am standing in line to brush my teeth … I wake up in my bed and everyone is getting ready. I can't stop shaking.

"Hey Wiggins, you ok man?" everyone surrounds me and is asking me questions. In without a doubt the weakest voice I'd used since I arrived to basic training "What happened?"

"Dude you blacked out in the latrine. We couldn't wake you up we had to carry your big ass back to the room."

"Shit man I gotta get ready," trying to pull myself out of bed.

"Naw man Drill Sergeant said take you to bed and keep you there till sick call. He's gonna tell our Drill Sergeant what happened. You're good" Private Rook informed me. Damn good deal I thought to myself as I slipped back out of consciousness. I'm awakened again a few moments later to the beautiful sound of Drill Sergeant Colons bellowing throughout the room "Why the fuck is Ranger Wiggins still in bed?!" Evidently the Drill Sergeant on duty at the time of my recent demise failed to inform my D.I. as he said he would … big surprise. I felt it best just to remain "unconscious" and let my battle buddies tell the story.

I to this day do not remember the next 24 hours, but suddenly I was awake in a hospital bed with my female D.I. standing over me telling me I owe her for bringing my hygiene kit and a change of clothes. Partly trying to play dumb and partly completely lost I asked her what was going on. Drill Sergeant Whittfield then informed me that I had been in the hospital for two days, and anyone who misses seventy-two hours of training was to go through basic training all over again. Not to mention tomorrow was qualification day. This was my worst nightmare. I was almost done! I mean I had a lot of fun but it was nothing that I wanted to do again! I was in and out of consciousness for the rest of that day though I finally got warm and was feeling a lot better including feeling completely rested for the first time in weeks. Approaching seventy-two hours the doctor came in to see me to give me my diagnosis.

"Well from the looks of your hands I'd say you have a case of mild frostbite." I looked at my hands for the first time to realize the skin was peeling off of both hands completely; it looked bad but didn't hurt at all. The doctor took my temperature "Well you still have a 102 degree fever, what do you wanna do?"

"Hey doc is it true if you miss seventy-two hours of training you have to redo basic?" I asked, hoping for "the truth." The truth is what I got. "That's right soldier." At this point I began begging him to release me, assuring him I felt much better. He finally agreed to let me back to my company on light duty.

I rejoined my company with one hour left of

qualification on the M-16. Upon arriving I reported to Drill Sergeant Grubb who was my meanest Drill Sergeant by far. Handing him my orders of light duty I assured him I was good to go to which he replied, "Get your damn rifle and get out there!" In a moment of relief I dashed off to locate my rifle. My relief disappeared a few minutes later when I realized it was snowing like crazy. Practically everyone was done qualifying except a few losers who would just never get it no matter how hard they tried. As it had turned out it had not snowed since the night before but there was a lot of snow on the ground and now it seemed to be an all out blizzard. I could barely make out the targets popping up and down from seventy-five meters to three hundred meters and on top of that I had snow landing in my sights and I couldn't quit sneezing … it seemed hopeless! As I readied myself and my weapon I remember thinking come on Wiggins you're the best out here you've already proved it just do the damn thing and be done with it! Whether it was fear of failing or the cold I will never know as I stood there shaking while being rodded onto the range. When a shooter enters or exits a range he must be rodded on or off to make sure that the weapon is clear. The rodder simply runs a steel rod down the barrel of the weapon to make sure that nothing is in it. Then over the speaker came the words "lock and load and watch your lane." Moment of truth boys, as the targets started popping up and I started dropping them. I missed my first target halfway through the exercise, "oh well, there goes my perfect score but I can still get expert." And then it happened, a rarity, two targets popped up one at 100 meters and one

36

at 150 meters perfectly aligned, and if you aim just right high enough but not too high, you can kill two birds with one stone. And that's just what I did. 40 out of 40 the Ranger standard, in a snow storm, and sick as hell! It's my story and I will tell it how I want!

W.A.R. in the Ozark Mountains

Ok, I know you didn't buy this book to read about basic training in Missouri, so I will end my tales of basic training with one last story. Land navigation week in the Ozark Mountains. Now this is what I signed up for. Just you, a compass, a map and the wild outdoors. In what I considered the best week of basic training we spent the week learning every type of land feature, learning our pace count, and then putting the knowledge to use. Friday, was the day we tested what we had learned. I was not worried at all, of course, because I have excelled in land nav. and planned on doing the entire course running. The land nav. instructor handed out maps, alcohol pens, compasses, and grid coordinates while giving us our instructions.

"On this course you will not cross any paved roads. If you cross a paved road you are off the course and need to replot. You may use the straight line method or the curve method (which is usually used to keep you on trails). Under no circumstances is anyone to climb any cliffs or swim any rivers!" instructed the course manager. As he reached into the box to hand me my set of grid locations he quickly looked up, "Oh you're my Ranger aren't you?!"

"Not yet sergeant!" I bellowed back in desperation.

"Well you're in luck. We put together a special course for 3rd Ranger Batt. a few years ago. When I'm done with these soldiers I will go in the office and find your course." Oh great, I thought to myself the shit never ends. It was 1100hrs and we had 6 hours to finish the course and everyone was already on the move except for me. This was killing me because I wanted to be the first one done. "Ok Wiggins, here's your set of points there are only three (everyone else had 6) but your course is ten times harder in that the points are all on different sides of the course with no points in the middle to check your position. Plot carefully and remember NO dangerous stuff."

"Roger Sergeant" long sigggggghhh.

Drill Sergeant Colon grining "Hey Ranger Wiggins you better be the first person back!"

So I took off about 30 minutes behind everyone else. Up and down, up and down, at least there are a lot of landmarks to go by I thought to myself. I had been perfecting my run pace all week, which no one else had done and every time I got the chance I was jogging. I found the first two points within an hour and a half which I thought was really good. They were pretty easy to find, but it was winter and all the bushes and whatnot were dead, making it fairly easy to spot any man-made contraptions. Well I had my first two points, point W and point R. One to go, I thought, as I started down the ravine only about two thousand meters to my last point. Ha, only I bet everyone else's six points didn't total up to two thousand meters! And then I reached it. I didn't even notice it on the map when plotting. A cliff, straight up, I looked left and then right then left again. It seemed never-ending. The cliff was only about thirty feet high but it was STEEP! After taking a rest to drink water and think for a few minutes, I decided to climb; it was the only way. I could literally see the point from the bottom of the cliff, but there was no way to make out what letter was on the sign. What I'd give for some binoculars right now. The first ten feet were the hardest and I was tiring quickly, cursing myself for running so much. I grasped for shrubbery and roots clinging for dear life. I flung my left arm up for a pretty thick and sturdy looking root that was inviting me for use, but when I grabbed it and found it was attached to nothing, I slipped. I was only about 20 ft. up but man for a split second it felt like I was falling from the Empire State Building. I grabbed a hold of another root that saved me from impact but another root caught my face. I lowered myself to the ground. Dammit! I cursed myself. By this time my face was bleeding pretty badly so I ripped my shirt and applied pressure. It quickly soaked. I wasn't worried about it. All I could think about was how the hell was I gonna get to the top of the cliff.

After about twenty minutes of rest I decided to make another crack at it. I thought hell, I'm 6'5", if I get a running headstart and jump that will knock out a pretty good hunk of it. Amazingly enough I was actually right. After the jump it seemed as though I was halfway up, and with this encouragement I began climbing. This time seemed much easier; I think it was a little desperation and rest that gave me the extra boost. Within a minute I reached the top and had my final point. Have you guessed what it was yet? Yup, A, my three points spelled out WAR. If I had half a brain I would have realized this and saved myself a lot of headache and hard work with that damn cliff. But the feeling of complete stupidity ended very quickly as I realized that the last point was within one hundred meters of the road that led straight back to my starting point. Forgetting the pain and fatigue I began to run, not jog, run. I had thirteen hundred meters to the starting point and fifteen minutes till I reached three hours. I was certain no one had finished yet.

As I approached the cabin running, Drill Sergeant Colon and the instructor came running out "What the hell happened?"

I slowed to a walk, gasping for air, trying to get at an altered state of parade rest "what do you mean Drill Sergeant? I'm finished."

One screamed "no your not" and the other yelled "what happened to your face?" the two sergeants barraged me with questions.

"The three points spell WAR and I had a little fall."

"Where did you fall Wiggins?" my Drill Sergeant asked.

I hesitated…"uh I was running with a walking stick and fell and it caught my face."

"Goddamn Wiggins you almost lost you eye dumbass!" bellowed D.I. Colon.

"Wiggins you climbed a cliff didn't you?" the instructor asked. Before another lie could come out of my mouth thank goodness, the instructor informed me that the only way to get the last point was in fact to climb the cliff. I admitted my "mistake" and awaited my punishment, but the instructor walked up and slapped me on the back and said "damn god job Wiggins you beat the course record no one has ever completed the course in less than 4 hours. How did you do it?" I simply told him I wanted to be the first back so I ran most of it and got a little lucky. Plus I didn't really hesitate and look for an alternative to climbing the cliff. And for the first time I truly realized that it was possible...I was gonna be a Ranger!

So I was back in the hospital getting my face cleaned up and looked after. The doctor said he didn't think I needed stitches and gave me a salve to put on my wound whenever it started to get dry. He did assure me that I would have a pretty nice scar and again informed me how close I was to losing an eye. I finally got to see the wound in the mirror and boy were they right, less than an 16th of an inch I'd say. It was nasty. On the walk back to the barracks I thought of the letter I would write home telling of how I got my new scar jumping out of a helicopter. I never sent that story home and it was a good thing too, as the wound healed completely and left no scar...I still had my chance to be on the cover of Esquire magazine some day!

Ok so that's the end of my shortened highlight reel of basic training!

Airborne...R.I.P.

"Free at last free at last praise God almighty we're free at last." This is what described my bus ride from Missouri to Ft. Benning, Ga. We were set to arrive at airborne school Friday afternoon, just long enough to get our stuff situated and then we were free for the weekend. Wait, did I hear this right? "Free?" What exactly does free mean? Like free to roam around post but if you leave it's the gallows for you?! Yes I had heard right, we could actually do anything we wanted.

"Let's get fucked up!!" roared one of the Herrington brothers in excitement. I agreed it sounded like a good plan except for two things. First being I wasn't 21 yet and secondly my car was only hours away. I convinced the Herrington brothers to chip in for my Greyhound bus ticket and I would go home to retrieve my car and return to base (RTB) before Monday, saving us hundreds of dollars in cab fares in the weeks to come.

I didn't really get to see my family that weekend. Someone merely met me at the Greyhound station and gave me my car and I drove straight back. I would return a few weeks later for my best friend Carlos' wedding...hopefully Airborne!

Airborne school was completely different than basic training. In my class there were all types of trainees ranging from Colonel's to cadets from ROTC in college. Most of these cadets thought that they were already officers and could order us around, but they found out the hard way that wasn't true. One airborne instructor was Ranger qualified and used to be in Battalion, and one day he noticed one of the cadets was wearing a Ranger Challenge Tab. He walked up to the cadet and yelled in his face "what Ranger did you challenge?" All I could think was damn that was bad ass!

The first week was mostly PT and quickly weeded out a lot of high ranking personnel. Everywhere you go in airborne school you are required to run, in addition to the fairly intense PT and demanding training schedule. The days begin at 0530hrs and usually end around 1700hrs and every minute of it is used to the fullest.

The first week is known as ground week, and as I mentioned before, there is a lot of PT during this week. During this week you also complete what is called the swing –land trainer. And just my luck, my stick leader was affectionately known by the other blackhats as the swing-land trainer Nazi. A stick is a squad that you jump out of an airplane with and a blackhat is an airborne instructor. They are called a Blackhat because they actually wear black hats.

The Swing-Land Trainer Nazi

The perfect landing, according to the US Military, is when your body hits the ground in this order; feet, calves, thighs, buttocks, and pull up muscle. It's much harder than it sounds! If you ask me any landing in which you survive is a perfect landing. So with the swing-land trainer, the jumper jumps off of a plank 20 feet up with a cable hooked to the jumper's harness and the blackhat swings you until he decides to drop you at which time you must perform a perfect landing. Well my blackhat swore that he didn't need to see anyone land. He could tell by the imprint left in the gravel if a correct landing was performed. Every other stick in the company had moved on to the next training exercise and there was my stick...still swinging. We swung for two days and only maybe 3 people had passed the exercise. "Wiggins you fall like a rock! You're gonna kill yourself!" the blackhat would yell every time. The swing-land Nazi was going to fail the entire stick if we didn't pass by the end of the week. Here I was certain that I could pass Ranger training, but honestly did not think that I was gonna pass airborne school. Then on the third day as it turned out, the swing-land Nazi had a dental appointment and surprise, surprise, my entire stick passed within an hour. When the swing-land Nazi returned from his appointment in the afternoon to find us all at the exit door tower, all he said was "you lucky bastards." I felt lucky!

The Mock Tower

The mock exit tower is the second most fun part of airborne school. It is a 30ft. tower from which you must properly execute a jump. When out of the tower you glide down a three hundred foot zip line and must maintain composure the entire time. Seems easy enough right? Unfortunately, for some people every jump is a night jump, meaning people tend to close their eyes when jumping from high elevations, and that is a no go. Personally the higher up I am, the better I perform. I love heights.

Jump Towers

The second week the PT continues but the focus is on the infamous towers. Anytime you enter or leave the barracks you must complete 10 pull ups. This is to get you as ready as possible to perform slips, which makes you change direction when parachuting which could be the difference between life and death. Tower week has since been tossed out of airborne school due to fatalities. There were originally plans to tear the towers down, but they were quickly scrapped due to the symbolic nature of them. What happens when you experience the tower is you get drawn in a parachute to the top of the tower (300ft) and then it drops you, so basically it's a practice jump, without the jump. The problem is if the wind blows there is a chance of getting blown back into the tower which could be fatal. In my jump class a small girl was blown into the tower and died. It was a sad day for airborne school, and I believe my class was the last to use the towers though I'm not 100% sure.

My jump class

Jump Week

Finally, if you have made it through the first two grueling weeks, you will enter jump week in which you will experience five jumps including one night jump. Live through those and you are now airborne. This is your new job. And one day you may make a jump where you have enemy combatants on the ground shooting at you. Talk about intense. Why would anyone ever want to do anything else in life?! While in Battalion I would make a lot of jumps, mostly in the States, some in other countries. A couple in war?

Ranger Training

Finally here! The Ranger Indoctrination Program (R.I.P.). Down to the elite now, three time volunteers, only people who want to be here are here. No more snot-nosed kids who joined the Army for college money, and no room for whiners. Should get interesting. There are about twelve of us standing outside the airborne barracks waiting for the Ranger Instructors (R.I.'s) to show up. It was very obvious that everyone is nervous. We have all heard nothing but horror stories about Ranger training since day one. I was about to have my first.

"Hey you maggots, get your hands out of your pockets. You got one minute to get all of your bags on the truck except keep one duffel...Why in the hell are you still standing there, MOVE! Form it up let's see what I'm dealing with here. You three make a separate formation." Baca, Robinson, and I quickly made a separate formation. "One of you maggots wanna tell me why you didn't get hair cuts?"

I replied "We did sergeant, Airborne."

"What the fuck?! First of all am I wearing a blackhat? The next person who calls me Sergeant Airborne will rue the day he was born! When did you get that haircut?" asked the R.I.

"Yesterday Sergeant, Air..." Shit we have been calling our airborne instructors Sergeant Airborne for the last three weeks!

"You knew you were getting picked up today you should have gotten it this morning!" shouted the R.I. "Look closely men, I can promise you these three over here will not be with you at graduation. If any of you at all graduate. Here's what's gonna happen. We are gonna take a little run to the R.I.P. barracks and you are gonna square away your shit. Chow formation is at 1700hrs and tomorrow you start training. Get your duffles on, let's go!" That "little run" was only about two miles thank God, but with my 65lbs. duffle it sure seemed farther. Well I made it through my first experience with an R.I. and I learned something. Evidently Ranger's invented the Army fuck fuck game.

I was in bed at 2030hrs that night. The next day was the PT test and I was a little worried. To continue on in the R.I.P. course you have to score at least a perfect 300 by Army standards and spell the word Ranger...in pull-ups. For those of you who aren't mathematicians, that's six pull-ups. The mistake most R.I.P. attendees make during airborne school is it's the first time they've been "free" in months, so they tend to party a lot more than they should considering what they are trying to accomplish, and I was one of them.

At 0530hrs two hundred and forty seven soldiers formed up. In less than two hours it will be half that, the worst part...we all know it. And here we go, the R.I.'s come out screaming about how messy the barracks are and before we know it we are being smoked. To be smoked is to be pushed as far as you physically can until the point it at least seems that you can do no more. As I'm doing push-ups I'm thinking they can't be giving us a PT test today if they are smoking us. The regular Army doesn't work that way. My thoughts are interrupted by "Get on you feet and line up at the pull up bars." I'm completely confused at this point. I thought the PT test started with push-ups…yeah we can't be having a PT test today. They are just screwing with us. After what seemed like about an hour smoke session, the R.I.'s marched us to the PT field for the PT test. My initial thought was man, this isn't fair, but as I learned quickly in R.I.P., they don't care about fair.

The first event was the push-up. A correct push-up is lowering yourself to the ground till your chin and chest touch the ground and lifting yourself back up till your arms are fully extended while keeping your back perfectly straight. "Incorrect push-ups will not count!" Famous last words. My grader for the day was Staff Sgt. Billings. Sgt. Billings had been voted asshole R.I. for every class two years running. He had an incident during a jump in which his arm got tangled in the static line and he almost had his arm ripped off. He could no longer serve on the line and was moved to the training battalion. He was always telling stories about '93 in Somalia. It was very obvious he was bitter and liked to take it out on us.

"Front lean and rest position….begin!" I'm pumping them out; I know it could all end right here. I'm doing much better than I expected after the smoking we just got. Then I get to 47 and I swear to God I hear the number 47 for eight push-ups in a row. There's no hope, it's over…finally 48, 49, 50… Ok now we are back on track but my 2 minutes is nearing an end 69, 70, 71. I'm reaching muscle failure. SGT. Billings is laughing, "Your Jello Wiggins you're done." I position myself in the up rest position, twenty seconds left I'm at 79 and I need 81 push-ups to pass. Ten seconds to go I struggle to get one out, I make it that's 80. The count down begins 7..6...5..4..3... it's like something you see in a movie. I let out a scream and drive the last one home. Time up. I collapse. By the skin of my teeth, wow.

Next event was the sit-up. A correct sit-up will be graded as follows: starting position on your back, knees at a 90 degree angle, feet always remain flat on ground, and hands always remained interlocked behind your head. You will bring your body to an upright position and then lower it again. If the grader does not feel you came to a complete upright position the sit-up does not count. Well we didn't get smoked in this area earlier, so I should have no problem. I was right. I reached 81 sit-ups with plenty of time to spare and decided it was best to keep going. I wound up doing around 90 sit-ups in the two minutes allotted. I had learned not to quit just because you reach the max number they grade for in basic training; I could only imagine what would have happened if I had done that during this PT test.

The next event was the two mile run. Again I would have no problem completing this event either. To successfully pass the 2 mile run you must complete it simply within 13 minutes. I had been running in the mountains for the last few months and had an advantage in this area. On Saturdays one of my drill sergeants would take the Herrington brothers and me on what he called the river run. The river run was 10 miles long half straight down to the river, and half straight up. I was one of the first to complete the run which shocked some of the R.I.'s because I definitely don't look like a runner. One R.I. even accused me of cheating, but another R.I. stuck up for me saying he watched me. I was honestly a little surprised that I didn't finish first, but I still finished with one of my best times at 10:59. The good thing about finishing first is I got to rest for a few minutes. I was afraid the smoking would start any minute but it didn't. When the rest of my group finished we then ran to the pull-up bars.

The pull-up. This exercise is started in the hanging position. When told to begin you must pull yourself up till your chin rests on top of the pull up bar then lower yourself back down until your arms are straight. There is no swinging or rocking yourself allowed you must remain "stiff" and controlled at all times. R-A-N-G-E-R, Ranger!!! 6 pull-ups, barely, and I drop. "What in the hell are you doing Wiggins?" shouts SGT. Billings. Not knowing what to say I spouted out, "Recovering sergeant."

"Well you'll have plenty of time to recover in Worldwide! You are supposed to complete 10 pull-ups!" OH SHIT…NOOOOO.

"SGT, I was confused I thought we only had to complete 6 pull-ups." I pleaded with SGT Billings.

Being the asshole that he is he tells me "should have paid closer attention you're S.O.L." (shit outta luck). I stand and watch the rest of the guys all complete their pull-ups with the worst feeling in my stomach. I was going to Worldwide. That meant I was no longer in Ranger training and would get shitty details till I received my orders for another unit, most likely in Korea. I was still standing there feeling sorry for myself when SGT. Billings told me to mount the bar. I was excited for another chance but also worried. As I stated earlier, pull-ups are not my strong point and to be honest it took all I had to complete the first six not to mention the pull-ups we had to do before the PT test. I guess it was sheer will power that enabled me to even get to 9 pull-ups but there was no way I could do another one. I dropped from the bar and cursed myself bitterly.

The first day my Ranger class was cut down to around 150, the guys who left us that day were in no case weak, and they were fully prepared for what was to come. Some of us just get lucky, like me. I thought for sure I was gone, and when they didn't call my name my first reaction was "So SGT Billings isn't the asshole he tries to come off as." He made a point to tell me later that it wasn't his call. As it turns out Regiment was in need of NBC guys, and as far as SGT. Billings knew I was the first one to ever come through R.I.P. As I always say, half the battle is showing up.

When we weren't being tested we were training or in the class room. Most of the training is in land navigation, hand to hand combat (Gracie), and fast roping. I did considerably well in the land navigation area as you could imagine, and there will be a short side story with that in a minute. As for hand to hand combat, that was not my strong point. Hand to hand in Regiment refers to Gracie style wrestling. The Gracie brothers are most well known in Ultimate Fighting Championship series, and they put together a program for the Rangers. I wasn't so good at it. I have always been and always will be a street fighter, and there is no punching in hand to hand training. It consists of a lot of technical skills and holds which are very fast and must be precise. Being the two biggest guys going through R.I.P. at the time, I got teamed up to

54

practice with Baca a lot.

I had gone through airborne school with Baca and kinda thought he was a dick head because he never wanted to party with us and he always was trying to square us away even when we felt we didn't need to be. I would learn that he was just playin' it smart because we got stationed together and let me tell you, that guy knows how to party. One time when we were in Africa, we had a night off and went drinking. I will never know why but Baca got drunk and left the bar walking down the street punching out windows in cars. He was finally stopped by a man with a gun and told to get on his knees. Somehow in the process Baca disarmed him and commenced to beating his ass. The U.S. embassy got involved and Baca was busted down to a private and lost a month's pay. He quickly got his rank back because he was one of the best Rangers I ever met. I'm sure you have figured out by now, Baca is huge. He wasn't taller than me, but he must have worked out since he was baby because he was my height and solid as a rock. So we were paired together for hand to hand and it sucked because even if I got him in a hold he was so strong I always knew that if he wanted to, he could get out of it. In the final competition I figured it would come down to him and I, and he would kick my ass. I was wrong. He got beat in the first round by a movie star. This guy was in the movie *Nightmare On Elm Street* and played in a lot of television shows and someone had recognized him and soon it got back to the R.I.'s. Needless to say they gave him shit about it, but it wasn't as bad as I expected. Baca lost to this guy. He had got him in a choke hold and Baca damn near passed out before he tapped.

My first opponent probably weighed 130lbs soakin' wet. At the time I was around 205lbs. so I just pinned him and sat on him. So for the final it came down to me and Mr. Hollywood. We went for about five minutes, and it seemed no one had the edge. But in the end he got me in that damn choke hold and looking back, I realize I was fine and I should have countered, but I freaked out and tapped. Guess you can't win 'em all.

The Rangers are well known for fast roping into missions as most of our missions do not call for the helicopter to touch down. However, the Rangers do not send their men to air assault school where the regular Army goes to learn about fast roping. So we incorporate the training into R.I.P. Learning to fast rope in the Rangers consists of exiting a 50 foot mock tower over and over again till you get the principles down then you move onto a helicopter and do what we call elevators. When doing elevators you board a helicopter and hover at 90feet, fast rope out, and when everyone is on the ground, you do it again and again. As I learned the hard way, it's important to control the rate speed at which you are roping with your feet or you will burn a hole in your leather gloves and end up with a huge blister.

The day after the PT test is the five mile run which you must complete within 40 minutes. I completed the run in a little over thirty two minutes and was again accused of cheating but I was getting used to that at this point. After the five mile run was the Combat Water Survival Test. There are three parts to this test, and the first is a 75 meter swim with all of your gear on and a weapon.

On the way out of the barracks, I was hurrying as always, and there was a soldier in front of me takin' his sweet frickin' time so I shoved him and said get the hell out of the way. As he turned around my heart dropped .... shit, it was a R.I. Perez! He just glared at me, I knew what he was doing, he was memorizing me!

"Ok everyone understand what you have to do? ... Ok good now everyone turn around. All of my strong swimmers about face front and center." Hey shoot, I'm a strong swimmer, I'm from Florida, I'm a beach bum, time to show my stuff! The swim begins and about five meters into it I find myself wondering if they had everyone else turn around so they can't see the different techniques or so they can't see me embarrass myself. With soldiers falling out left and right, I was beginning to think I was gonna drown myself. It didn't help that I kept going under, and when I'd resurface there was a R.I. throwing more water on top of me. My boots weighted 500lbs...apiece! The R.I.'s were taunting the whole way. "Wiggins you aint gonna make it want us to pull you out?" And then five meters from the end I felt the bottom I pushed off (because our feet weren't suppose to touch the bottom) and made one last effort for the finish line...made it. Suddenly a R.I. popped up from underwater, decked out in scuba gear "this guy touched the bottom." No sense in making excuses; I had touched the bottom.

"Caught ya red handed this time Wiggins, I knew you were cheating" an R.I. stated. Now I'm forced to make excuses.

"But sergeant I wasn't trying to cheat; my feet accidentally touched the bottom. I didn't know it was there" I exclaimed.

"Why didn't anyone else ACCIDENTALLY touch bottom then Wiggins" one R.I. asked. Well I had the obvious answer for that "No one else is over 6 foot sergeant." I guess I convinced someone or they just liked to give me a hard time. Either way they decided to let me retest. First I had to go to the practice pool and work on my technique which sucked because it was smoking me bad. Finally I got my second crack at the 75 meter swim and once again barely made it.

I was on my way to the second part of the CWST when I ran into R.I. "slow-ass" Perez again. My luck he remembered me and made me do flutter kicks in the water. Flutter kicks usually aren't that bad but then again you usually don't have your boots filled with water when doing them. When I reached the point that I could do no more flutter kicks, he had me do push-ups. Go down to the water blow bubbles back up then down to blow more bubbles again.

Finally I reached the second station. At this station the requirement was to drop from a high elevation into the water showing no sign of fear and resurface without losing any of your equipment. No problem at this station. In fact it kinda rejuvenated me by getting me pumped up. On to the last station to go...oh no guess who was the grader, my new buddy R.I. Perez.

While I was waiting in line for my turn to complete the last test R.I. Perez saw me and made me do more flutter kicks and push-ups while I waited. When it was finally my turn to do the exercise, R.I. Perez explained to me the procedure and then he told me to repeat it back to him.

Surprise, surprise, an Army fuck fuck game. "Sergeant I must jump from the platform, enter the water, and resurface without any gear on."

"Wrong, do push-ups; next," R.I. Perez said in a very sarcastic tone. I did push-ups till the guy behind me finished the exercise then I was told to recover. Again R.I. Perez told me the requirements for the exercise and told me to repeat them to him. I was wrong again. Flutter kicks goooooo. The next guy finished the exercise.

"Wiggins recover and get up here!" shouted R.I. Perez. "Now listen closely to me and repeat EXACTLY what I tell you." Ahhh now I get it. He wanted me to repeat to him word for word. I to this day still think I screwed it up, but I guess he was done havin' fun with me because he let me go finally. Ok PT test, complete. Five miler, done. CWST, check, what's next.

My favorite thing, a sixteen mile road march. With my long legs, I was built for road marchin'. This would be the longest road march I had completed. In basic training the longest road march we did was 12 miles with a 45lbs ruck, not long, but trust me, they trained me well. I was in charge of bringing up the rear and if anyone fell out they would fail the road march (which was required to pass basic) and so would I. You know this game by now. The road march was terrifically easy with breaks every half an hour, but still it was bound to happen, someone started lagging. Private Ortiz was a cute little girl that couldn't have weighed more than 85 pounds. I dunno what an 85lbs little girl is doing in the military, but here she was struggling with her 45 pound ruck. At first I took her ruck and strapped it on my front. But it was too late she was done. "Her feet hurt and she couldn't go on." In the end I wound up carrying her and her ruck the last couple of miles.

The big difference here was the pace. We had 3 hours to complete 16 miles. In some Ranger classes you aren't even allowed to run. Thank goodness we were. So with our 75lbs rucksack a marchin' we went. I was movin' out and makin' great time. I would run about 100 meters and then walk 100 meters; it seemed to be a good system. I ended up finishing 1st place by default. One guy finished ahead of me and he was a little guy. I was shocked. But he was disqualified because when they reweighed his ruck at the end of the march it wasn't 75lbs. He had made the mistake that many before him made and many after him would make. He calculated his water as a part of his 75lbs. and when he drank it all on the march that put him at around 70lbs, not acceptable. And the beginning of the march my ruck weighed 83lbs. and at the end it weighed 77lbs. So supposedly I drank about 6lbs. of water.

The training continued for weeks, but things seemed to lighten up a little for those of us left after those tests. Now we only had one test to go, the land navigation course. The land. nav. test was held at Cole Range. We had to spend a week at Cole Range training all day every day whether it be in a field wrestling around or perfecting our land nav. skills. We would practice land nav. at night and usually everyone would be back around 0100hrs. A couple of guys would get caught taking a nap against a tree, though I dunno how with all the wild bores and R.I.'s roaming around. Then the smoking would begin. "Hit the woodline!" the R.I. would yell. Then he would stand there with his night vision (N.O.D.S.) on watching for cheaters. It was pitch dark and people would run into each other and fall down. And after a while some people would even start walking, making it impossible to meet the time limit and turning us against each other. The worst was when the R.I. would be on the megaphone and when he said, "You're up," you had to run, and then he'd say, "He sees you you're down," at which point you have to hit the ground and low crawl. It was a real smoker. This would go on literally for hours. We had a total of two hours to sleep a night, thirty minutes of which you were guaranteed guard duty. It was awful to sleep anyway because you would just wake up tired and covered with dew and freezing.

I have never been as happy as I was to see the last day of Cole Range. In the afternoon the land nav. test began and was scheduled to run till midnight, at which time everyone must be back or you automatically failed. Nine points to find in six hours in the afternoon and nine more with the same amount of time at night. We were working in buddy teams of two. I don't remember the guy's name who was my "buddy," but I will never forget him. This guy was awful at land nav., but I wasn't worried I could do it all on my own. All he had to do was write down the points as I found them. But he was done ... he kept falling behind and I would have to wait on him to catch up. We had been told to stick together and not get separated at all, and under no circumstances were we to use roads. Well as I said, my buddy kept falling back and I got tired of waiting on him and I was really moving out. I stopped to take a break and wait for this douche to catch up, only he never did. I started to back track to look for him, I couldn't yell and draw attention to myself because there were R.I.'s on patrol making sure we were following the rules. A couple of guys, as every night, got caught propped up against a tree sleeping.

I came up on a small dirt road. After a moment of deliberating I decided to dash across it. Mistake, busted, you've got to be kidding me!

"Hey get over here! What are you doing on the road? Where is your Ranger buddy?" I was barraged with questions. I didn't have a good answer for any of them, only excuses.

"Sergeant I was merely crossing the road to find my Ranger buddy who fell behind." Not the right answer; push-up time. As I was getting smoked guess who showed up? That's right, my buddy. I was thinking about the ass whipping I wanted to give him when the R.I. started asking him the same questions to which he responded, "Ranger Wiggins left me behind and I was just looking for him." Oh man that son of a bitch is gonna get it when these R.I.'s let us go. Lucky him, the R.I.'s didn't like his excuses anymore than mine.

"Why were you falling behind private? Just do fucking push-ups!"

Finally the smoking was over and the Sergeants showed us their N.O.D.S. acting like we were buddies and then at the end they said "That's right, remember how cool they are. Spread it to the rest of your buddies and tell them if they cheat we will know." Right, whatever, I thought.

Now that I had completely lost my bearing I had to find a new point to plot from. This was extremely difficult under red light. Also this course was harder than the one in Missouri because there were not near as many landmarks to check myself with. Very easy to get lost. I finally found the last point and we bee-lined back to the base.

There were already a few people back, and to my surprise they were just sitting on their rucks. Wonder what that's about? Why aren't they being smoked? Why do I hear dogs barking? As I approached the R.I., not only did I find out why I heard dogs barking, but I made another unsettling discovery. There were about 4 five gallon buckets filled with empty beer bottles. R.I. Perez snatched our list of grid points out of my hand. I could tell he was wasted and his dogs were going nuts tied up next to him. These weren't cute little lap dogs; these were big mean Rottwielers. Now I'm not afraid of dogs at all, but I had a bad feeling we were going to be playing with them all night. "Another failure," SSG Perez laughed. "What?!" I blurted out. He showed me the sheet. Oh my God! My idiot Ranger buddy had for some reason not written down the last point, and copied one of the other points wrong. What could I say? The R.I.'s would only see any explaining as excuses.

"Go take a seat on your ruck with the rest of Worldwide" SSG Perez pointed to the rest of the gang.

It was about 2330hrs as I shuffled over to meet up with the rest of my Ranger buddies, 30 minutes till the games began. This would be the longest break I had had in weeks, but I couldn't enjoy it. Talking with the rest of the guys, very softly so that the R.I.'s couldn't hear us, I learned that not one of them had passed the course. As the last minutes dwindled away more and more guys were coming in and not a one of them got a GO.

Time for my ranger buddy who had completely ruined my night to screw me one last time. "Sergeant, can I hit the woodline I gotta take a shit?" this idiot yelled.

"Bring back proof on a stick!" the R.I.'s roared with laughter. "The rest of you do push-ups till he gets back!"

No one had passed the course, but I couldn't believe that they would fail all 17 of us who remained. And they didn't, although they were trying to let us believe we had all failed. I knew that we didn't because they smoked us till the sun came up the next day. If you quit or you fail, your through, no more games. By the way, private dumb ass brought back poop on a stick for the R.I.'s. We all paid for his mistake.

Now before we had left for Cole Range, which was the last step in the process of R.I.P. we all chipped in $2. Those of us who were left Friday morning would get two hot dogs, a snickers, and a coke. I was skeptical but there were the R.I.'s firing up the grill while we got some "much deserved rest." You're through they told us, you made it, you're a Ranger. Everyone anxiously devoured their food way to fast as we waited for the bus to come pick us up. At that point I was just happy to hear that we didn't have to walk back to the barracks. We had walked from the barracks to Cole Range and it was about 20 miles. I don't know if they play this trick on every class or if it was because we were still waiting on the bus and they were bored but the R.I.'s decided to smoke us one last time. Not five minutes after we had just finished eating the most food we had eaten all week, we were returning it. What started as 247 R.I.P. attendees ended with 17 and the next day we graduated and headed for our respected Battalions.

Operation Enduring Freedom:

O.E.F. 2

We were told that we are under no circumstances to ever talk to the public about Operation Anaconda. Hell, we aren't even supposed to discuss it with our families. OPSEC, which is Operation Security, has lightened up quite a bit especially now that there are so many conventional soldiers involved in the war. Unfortunately much of this mission is still classified though there has been a great book written on the mission titled *Not A Good Day To Die* by Sean Naylor a journalist for the *Army Times* who breaks all the rules. Sean Naylor is not in the service he is a columnist for the *Army Times*. All I want to do in my book is honor the Ranger's who paid the ultimate sacrifice on 4Mar2002.

SGT Bradley Crose
Cpl Matthew Commons
Spc. Marc Anderson

One for the Airborne Ranger in the sky!!!

O.E.F. 3

September 2002, 1st Ranger Battalion had just got back from a summer training mission in Seattle, Washington but there was no rest for the weary. After battling the non-stop rain in the northwest for the last three weeks, we were gearing up to head back to Afghanistan. The good part was we actually knew about this mission for about a month in advance so we had time to prepare ourselves and even a little leave. As it always is with a Special Operations unit, we were not permitted to tell anyone that we were leaving. In theory you are not even suppose to tell your wife anything. Of course someone would always get busted sending an email or making a call in reference to what was going on with the unit, not meaning to cause any harm, but spec. ops doesn't take any chances, and if you get caught violating OPSEC then your out of the unit. In later deployments we were allowed to tell spouses that we were deploying but not the actual date or where we were going.

After 27 hours on a C-17 we were finally entering Afghan airspace. It was the middle of the night in Kandahar, Afghanistan where we would be landing, so we couldn't see anything. We were told to strap in because the final approach would be very steep. The planes have to stay high until right at time to land to avoid RPG attacks. The lights went out and red lights started flashing. Whoa, what is this, reality T.V.? What's the deal with the flashing red lights? I still don't know to this day, but it was pretty intense. I was looking straight ahead as was everyone else on the plane, and you could see the look of uncertainty in the glow of the red light. It seemed like something was wrong with the plane, almost like we were going down. I mean, we were told to strap in, red lights were flashing, and we seemed to be falling like a rock. And finally it felt like we hit like a rock! When the plane came to a stop, it was the age old game of hurry up and wait. The back ramp of the plane opened and everyone was running frantically trying to get off. But then when we finally all got off, no one knew what to do, so we wound up taking a knee just outside the plane for over an hour. That's how the Army operates, hurry up and wait. Finally the P.A.X. (personnel) from 2nd Ranger Battalion whom we were replacing showed up and they got on our plane and we got on their Jinga Trucks. A Jinga Truck is middle eastern terminology for a big dump truck basically. They usually have chains skirting the entire truck that jingle when the truck moves: jingle truck?

There were about 30 Rangers in my group, and once we got to the compound it took a while to get set up. After we were all set up, we were told to get some shut eye, which I thought was ridiculous seeing as how I had just spent the last 27 hours on a plane resting. As it turned out, my group would spend the next three months as a Quick Reaction Force (Q.R.F.). It was not at all what I expected. Our last deployment to Afghanistan had landed us in the middle of some very intense fighting, and I expected the same this time. Maybe it was true maybe, the war in Afghanistan was coming to an end.

We got called up for Q.R.F. every now and again, but it would always turn out to be nothing, or the action would be over by the time we got there. This drummed up a lot of boredom. Due to the nature of our mission, ha, we were not allowed to call home or write letters which would have been nice for killing time. Instead I decided to keep a journal of what was going on, just to burn time. Finally about halfway through deployment, they allowed us one phone call home. Of course the call would be monitored. Now who the hell would I call?

Of all the people who were back home worrying about me, I made the mistake of calling my "high school sweetheart," if you could actually call her that. She affectionately went by the name Lola and was a piece of work let me tell ya, but I loved it. We had been kind of off and on for years, only when she got in the mood for me, I of course was for some reason in love with her. I grew very excited as the phone rang, I hoped she would answer.

"Hello?" the sexiest voice ever answered.

"Hey Lola, what's up?" I replied.

"Uh...not much...who is this?" she asked.

"It's Tom!" I replied excitedly. I was hoping this would be where the conversation picked up and she would be excited to hear from me. I was devastated to be so wrong.

"Oh hey, what's up" she replied, "I didn't recognize the phone number."

"Yeah this isn't my cell," I told her barely remembering I couldn't tell her I was in Afghanistan.

"So what have you been up to? I haven't heard from you in a while." she asked. Damn what in the hell was I supposed to tell her, my mind went blank. In the meantime she seemed to be holding a conversation with someone who was with her too.

"Oh nothing much" I replied stupidly "are you busy you sound busy?"

"Yeah actually I need to get back to class, can I call you later?" Lola asked completely unaware and uninterested. I just said no and hung up. I walked away from the little make shift phone booth with a new perspective. While I was there it was like I expected the world to stop spinning, and for me it had. But back home the world was very much spinning. Things were happening even though I wasn't there.

"Go get your shit on!" SGT Breeding screamed. And just like that everyone was moving out. We had set up a separate tent with all of our mission essential gear in it and had it ready to strap on at a moment's notice. Within five minutes twenty Rangers were geared up and anxiously awaiting at the chopper. The commander came out and gave us a very quick briefing.

"Ok men listen up! A small coalition compound located in the Skhin Valley has been assaulted. There were three people inside, all wounded. Number one priority is to get them out. Then secure the compound. Move out!"

Simple enough, I could handle that. Everyone was having small talk on the chopper ride to the compound, mostly asking each other who they thought was in the compound. Since it was only three people it most likely was not military. Unfortunately I will not be able to tell you who it was, but it doesn't really matter anyway. When we arrived the enemy was already long gone and we found the casualties. Two men dead with multiple wounds and one severely wounded. We called back the chopper that had been circling overhead to get the three men. The plan was for the chopper to RTB (return to base) and drop the casualties then come back for us before dawn, which was about four hours round trip.

My "get to the choppa!" picture!

Four hours came and went and my platoon sergeant, SFC Holmes, couldn't get an answer as to when we might be picked up. SFC Holmes was not one to sit around and soon we were on the move. He decided if we were gonna be there we might as well do something, so we went on patrol looking for the enemy that attacked the compound. We all knew good and well that the enemy was long gone. Afghan's move very quickly even through the roughest terrain. No matter how much we train, the fact is American soldiers are loaded down and move very slowly up and down the mountains and the locals know all the trails and move lightly and quickly. And so we walked and we walked no tracks, no broken branches, and no leads whatsoever.

I look over and I see one of my Ranger buddies standing at a tree fiddling in his pockets. Then he pulls out some change and tries to put it in the tree. Very curious, I walked over to him.

"Hey man what in the hell are you doing?" I asked.

He very calmly replied to me "I'm just buying a soda."

I was about to go inform my platoon sergeant when he fell back into formation. I just let it go for the time being. As we later found out one of the drugs that they give us called mephloquin has a side effect. It causes you to have strange dreams. Well when you don't sleep, you don't dream, and this is what happens. This is not an isolated event. Anyone you talk to who has taken this drug will tell you they had strange dreams. A couple of deployments later I would have another incident like this. This time the Ranger was low-crawling down the side of a mountain when suddenly he started putting rocks in his pockets. When I asked him what he was doing he told me he had found a potato field and was taking some to cook back at the compound. It's almost funny if it wasn't so serious.

We were still on patrol and all of us becoming very complacent. I was lost in thoughts of back home, probably Lola, when a shot rang out. I hit the ground and moved my selector from safe to semi. I was searching for a target but it was too late. Just that quick the fight was over. I had only heard maybe eight shots. SFC Holmes gave the all clear and we began to get to our feet. All of us were confused as to what had just happened. As it turned out, we had walked up on three Al-Qaeda, and SFC Holmes who was carrying a M4, slung it, drew out his M9(hand gun) and killed all three enemy PAX before anyone including the enemy knew what was going on. I now knew how easily complacency could get you killed, and I vowed to never lose focus again. You just never know.

Road side bombs and I.E.D.'s (Improvised Explosive Devices) are not the number one killer in Afghanistan and Iraq as many believe, complacency is. I know first hand after top gunning on a convoy for hours on end it's very easy to let your mind wander. My guess is ninety percent of all I.E.D. incidences could be avoided if soldiers would pay better attention. An I.E.D., in most cases, can be easily spotted by the top gunner of a vehicle. However top gunners are taught that their primary job is to scan for would be attackers and tend to leave the road to the driver and T.C. (Tank Commander). It is much more difficult for the top gunners in Afghanistan as they must scan the ridgeline of very high mountains for ambushes. In Iraq, except for the buildings in Baghdad, the gunner can see for a long distances leaving more time to check the road.

SFC Homes reported what had happened to higher, and they were upset, if you can believe, that we had even left the perimeter of the compound. He was instructed to return and wait for pick up. We had walked probably eight to ten miles so it was gonna be a while before we got back. SFC Holmes had agreed to return to the pick up point but he however had said nothing about taking the same route. Our ten mile route back turned into fifteen very easily. And it just so happened that our route found us quite possibly the rest of the trios gang.

We were walking past this cave and you could hear voices inside plain as day. Why would anyone be inside a cave during the day unless they were hiding? Assuming that it was the enemy inside, SFC Holmes radioed to higher asking permission to enter the cave and apprehend the people inside. Request denied!!! What in he hell is wrong with these officers? Most likely the bastards responsible for the killing of three Americans in the last 24 hours are holed up inside this cave and they are saying we can't go in because caves are dangerous. After deliberating for ohhhh about 1 minute, SFC Holmes came up with an alternate idea. He had the two squads get in the prone all with sights on the cave. Then he fired a round into the cave. There was a second of silence followed by about 50 rounds coming from the cave, but no bad guys. We were certain at this point that these were our guys. But they weren't emerging from the cave. Time to put the second part of SFC Holmes' plan into action. SFC Holmes on one side of the opening and SGT Wood on the other side directed the rest on the Ranger's to move further down the mountain. "Frag out!!!" they both yelled and threw their grenades into the cave with four seconds to put as much distance as possible between themselves and the cave. A tremendous explosion literally shook the ground so hard I couldn't help but wonder if the cave actually ran under us. At this point we were all ready to run if there was an avalanche, thank God there wasn't. We very carefully re-approached the cave and could hear whimpers inside. Who knows they may be faking it to fool us. For safe measures we tossed two more grenades in there and then went on our way. SFC Holmes became my hero that day!

We arrived back at the compound late that night and word was that we would have a chopper first light in the morning. Oh good, still no sleep. The chopper was a couple of hours late, but at least we got the hell out of there. A few days later it got out to higher about what SFC Holmes had done. Word was when we returned to the states he would be demoted to SPC and kicked out of the Rangers. Bullshit we all thought, complete bullshit.

The day after we returned everyone was doing routine maintenance on their weapons, which is typical especially after going on patrol. There was this one fairly new private who didn't seem to be the brightest crayon in the box. We had been at a range just before we left and he was loading mags for his gunner and for some reason no matter how hard he tried just could not get the last couple ofround into the mag. When he showed his gunner, the gunner freaked out on him and with good reason. This private had somehow loaded all of the 9mm rounds into the mag backwards and the last couple of course would not go in. Somehow, someway, he didn't get kicked out of the Rangers for it.

So this brain dead Ranger is cleaning his weapon and he has been assigned the M203. The M203 is a grenade launcher that attaches to the bottom of the M4 assault rifle. So I guess forgetting that he had loaded a round in the chamber of his M203 he squeezed the trigger without clearing the chamber. WOOSH!!! That was all we heard, but everyone heard it. We all looked up. "What in the hell was that!" we all exclaimed seemingly at the same time. The jackass private didn't even warn us. A few seconds later BOOM!!! It was a ways off but we all knew immediately it was friendly fire. Everyone jumped to go see what it hit! The grenade had hit an Afgani Pepsi truck. No one was hurt but the truck was destroyed and we defiantly wouldn't be having Pepsi anytime soon. The Ranger knew that he would be released for standards (RFS'd) now, and so did everyone else. We all just gave him so much shit for taking out our Pepsi supply.

The Rangers did get one fun mission on this deployment. The down side is the plan called for a small portion of the 82nd Airborne to operate with us as we did not have enough personnel. So the Rangers spent two days getting these Airborne guys up to speed. We had to go through all of their gear and make sure it was good to go, it was a little ridiculous. The NCOIC (non-commissioned officer in charge) was hilarious. He had put out the rule that there was to be no personnel effects included in soldiers gear for the mission. So he went around collecting all of these soldiers personnel gear in a bag.

One soldier had a bunch of letters on him from his girlfriend back home. The NCOIC took the bag of personal gear into another room, and emerged a few minutes later laughing his ass off, letters in hand. It was a dick thing to do but very funny at the time. He read two of the letters in entirety in a very feminine voice. It was a very descriptive dialogue of all of the "things" his girlfriend

78

couldn't wait to do to him when he got home. The Rangers were in tears laughing along with some of the 82nd, but this was not a group that got along very well in the first place, and the situation just added tension.

This mission had the group jumping onto the Iranian border. It seemed like no one was sure what the exact mission was. It mainly just seemed like a show of force, and that it would be. Approximately one hundred PAX jumped that day and one person got shot … a janitor, with a broom stick in his hand. What a joke.

My group left Kandahar in November and ventured up to Baghram Air Field which is the main base in Afghanistan. When we arrived, we learned that the rest of the battalion had returned to the states. Even more interesting was that supposedly they returned to the states because we were getting ready to go to war with Iraq. Yeah right!

We were allowed to mail letters at this point because they wouldn't even reach home before we did, which was silly. I took a big risk and opted to mail the journal that I had been keeping to Lola for safe keeping till I arrived. If I had been caught with it while trying to leave the country there might have been reprimands, but if they found I had mailed it to civilians there definitely would have been trouble. But I slipped through the cracks. I slipped something else through customs too! When I was ordered to check the body of one of the three men SFC Holmes had killed on the mountain, I had found an assassin pen with bullets. It is .25 caliber and sits on my book shelf as I write this. When I returned home I actually had the balls to fire a couple of rounds out of it. Fully aware that this ancient looking weapon could very easily blow up in my hand, I was sure to wear leather gloves. It shot as though I had just bought it. I fired two rounds and kept the other two as keepsakes because they have Arabic writing on them.

After not even quite three months deployed in Afghanistan I was home. As I stepped off of the plane onto the never so beautiful asphalt, I literally knelt down and kissed it. I really don't know how the regular army does it. Sure their missions aren't as intense as ours, but I don't think I could take being in either one of those countries for 18 months straight.

Of course we got leave soon after returning home, just long enough to let our families see that we were ok. My friends threw a nice welcome home party for me. Lola showed up around midnight, long after I was already drunk, which was her first mistake. After being there for only about twenty minutes and acting as though nothing was wrong, she informed me she had to leave. I begged her to stay but she said "I cant I'm seeing someone." And that stopped the party. We had been here before, more than once, and it's never been pretty. I was wasted and I think there was a lot of other stuff built up inside, but that night I had a total break down.

I said in a very polite manner "Yeah it's probably best if you leave, right now." As she walked out the front door, I walked out the back onto the balcony of Lance's second floor apartment. He had just gotten a new refrigerator and his old one was sitting there, and for some reason I picked it up and threw it from the balcony while screaming. At this point pretty much everyone was scattering. I began walking downstairs and Lance being the great friend that he is, caught up and walked with me.

"Where ya goin?" Lance asked.

"I wanna go for a drive." I responded.

"You sure that's such a good idea, you're pretty fucked up" Lance reminded me.

"Who fuckin cares." I said like I didn't have a care in the world. I was talking crazy and Lance was gonna make sure I didn't do anything to crazy.

"Well I'm goin with ya." Lance said nervously.

"Get in." I peeled out of the parking lot.

I didn't realize it at the time but Lola had pulled out right in front of me and I hauled ass out behind her so she must have thought I was chasing her. I peeled out into the street and was picking up speed rapidly. Thank God I had Lance with me as he pointed out two cops sitting in the road up ahead. I would have had a DUI for sure. I pulled into some apartment complexes and parked. Lance and I just sat there. To protect my pride, somewhat, I wont tell you what all happened in that parking lot that night, but I had a complete breakdown.

The next morning I was still very drunk and everyone else was still asleep. The night before I remember Lola telling me she had gotten my journal and had it at her house and said I could stop by and pick it up. So I packed a few beers and took a ride. I showed up at her place with half a beer in hand and surprisingly she let me in. She handed me my journal and apologized again. I'm not totally sure what she was apologizing for. At that point I just said, "look we can't be friends anymore." It was hard to say, I had known the girl for a long time, but I knew it had to happen. As I was leaving, a SUV pulled up in front of the house and the guy just sat there in the passenger seat seemingly waiting for me to leave. As I got one foot inside my car it hit me, this must be the guy. I slammed my door and walked back to his vehicle. Knocking on the window I was yelling "who are you?!" He was trying so hard not to make eye contact. That son of a bitch! By this time Lola and her mom were standing in the front yard and Lola's mom yelled "if you don't leave we are going to call the cops." Shit! Now what? I got in my car and peeled off.

I was contemplating circling the block and going back to the house but then what. And just then another friend from the past saved me. As I came screaming around the corner my car almost on two wheels John came running into the street. I parked the car right there in the street and walked inside with John and told him the entire story.

Of course I would wind up talking to Lola again in just a matter of a few weeks. I'm cursed for life, what can I say? We keep in touch but she basically has no part in my life anymore; even so, it's ironic that she affects everything that I do every single day.

Here I stand with roses
Outside her apartment door
It's seemed as though forever
Been gone fightin' a war
As I stand outside the door
Waiting to make up for lost time
Not expecting lost love
Or what I was about to find
I imagine what her expression will be
One of a loving surprise?
Never did I guess
There'd be another guy
So I knock on the door
And I hear a fumbling inside
I stand up a little taller
Like any "war hero" full of pride
As the door slowly opens
We both share a tear
She clings tightly to me
And whispers in my ear
I'm sorry I didn't know
God it's been so long
Everything's gonna be alright I say
But something seemed so wrong
Then I hear "honey who is it"
As he steps into the light
And everything I ever had was gone
Even the urge to fight
I slowly take a step back
The roses fall from my hand
I don't know what to do
This wasn't part of the plan
My vision blurs up and I can hear nothing
As she tries to explain
My knees become weak, I can hardly breath
I've never felt such pain
My minds racing a million miles a minute
Wondering how and why
I spent so long trying to stay alive
Now I just wish I could die
I manage to utter I'm happy for you
Then slowly turned to walk away
Waiting for her to grab my arm
And beg me to please stay
But reality hit
As I finally reached my car
My thoughts running wild
I've never been pushed so far
I could kill them both
But would that make me feel better
I want her to know the pain I felt
That's why I wrote this goodbye letter
God I loved you so much
I'm sorry it came to this
I can't live without you
I hope you found your happiness
I hope this proves I'd have done anything for you
And just how far in love I fell
I know we'll be together again one day
In the fiery pits of hell!

Operation Iraqi Freedom:

O.I.F.

Over the next few months the rumors grew about a war coming in Iraq. Though the day I arrived to Battalion I was expected to be an infantryman, I was now expected to be a chemical soldier. I was ordered to get all of my equipment ready "just in case." This task was near impossible as new chemical equipment was arriving every day. The other Rangers saw this. They also knew that they had never once had chemical training in their entire career. Now it seemed as though the entire training calendar was full of it. All of the guys started bugging me on a daily basis, but the truth of the matter was I didn't know any more than they did, which wasn't much.

It's hard to train soldiers who don't really care if they live or die on how to properly use military NBC equipment especially when they don't believe it will save them anyway. This is what Ranger Mason and I was asked to do. We knew from first hand experience that it works. While going through NBC school one of the exercises consists of wearing the chemical protective gear while placing five drops of VX (very lethal nerve agent) on a piece of metal then a live rabbit is brought into the room. Even though only five drops of VX from a syringe is placed, not even on the rabbit, with in five minutes the rabbit is convulsing, and a few minutes later is dead. This exercise is to prove to the NBC soldier that the protective gear does in fact work.

Finally I got the word, get a final count of all my gear, and issue two chemical suits to every Ranger. Well that's it, we are for sure going. Ranger Mason and I started attending meetings with all of the Battalions high ranking personnel which was a bit strange as we were only Specialist's but we were the NBC NCO's, so we had to be there. Then one day we got a date, Feb. 27, 2003 was the go date and no one outside the room was to know. Damn, that's a big piece of information to have. It's not fair that all these high ranking officers get to say goodbye to their wives but the enlisted guys get the shaft. I used that reason as justification for telling my Ranger buddies. Not that it mattered. No one seemed to believe me anyway. Even though they had been bugging me about it for weeks.

On Feb. 27, 2003 there was a formation. They took everyone's cell phone then we picked up our bags and headed for the plane. Just like that, no warnings, no goodbyes, everyone knew it was a part of the job I guess. I felt for the wives who would be sitting home wondering where their husband was that night. On the plane each Ranger got to submit one address for Battalion to send a letter to explaining to the recipient that we had been deployed in support of the Global War on Terrorism. When we were over the Atlantic they finally told us where we were headed, Saudi Arabia.

The entire conventional military would build up in Kuwait while almost every spec ops. unit would prepare in Saudi. We were literally right on the Iraqi border. I could easily see into Iraq from my tent. Our command told us that not even the

Saudi government knew that we were there, but I found that hard to believe. Just a few days after I had been there, quite possibly, the first combat related death of Operation Iraqi Freedom occurred. Master Sergeant Andy Fernandez was in 1st Ranger Battalion for years and years but had just made Delta Force a few weeks prior. He had a newborn child at home and the loss set very heavy with 1st Battalion. Every year 1st Ranger Battalion holds a Golf Invitational and all of the proceeds go into a fund for Andy's child's education.

My Ranger group had been in Saudi for about two weeks and had set up a nice little camp. The entire camp probably consisted of one hundred or so tents. In the compound there ranged everything from Rangers to Delta to SEALs and we had even brought in a small group from the 82nd Airborne for support. One day as I was tending to my NBC duties, and trying to hurry because dusk was coming quickly, I ran into the Herrington brothers who I had gone all the way from Basic Training through R.I.P. with. Shocked to run into each other we agreed to meet up later that evening in the same spot, when our duties were finished.

"Damn, I hope you guys are having as much fun as I am trying to get these Rangers trained up on NBC," I stated.

Brett said "Ha, I gave up on that week's ago."

"Hey we gotta run an errand wanna go with us?" Trinity asked.

"Sure," I said figuring what else did I have to do. In hindsight I should have known better. The Herrington brothers are trouble. Had all three of us been stationed together, as they wanted, there is no doubt in my mind we would all be sitting in

Leavenworth right now. As we were walking and bullshitting about old times I started to realize we were moving a pretty good ways from the compound. "Hey, where are we going?" I asked.

"Oh just over to the next town," Brett said ever so casually.

"What?!" I exclaimed. "Can we do that? I thought that no one is supposed to know we are here." The Herrington brothers just laughed and shrugged it off. If I had half a brain I would have turned around and returned to camp, but sheer curiosity inspired me to continue. After around an hour walk in the complete darkness we approached a few small buildings with lights on. Guess where we were heading. Straight to them. "This is insane" I thought as we entered one of the buildings.

Two locals were sitting at a table chatting, to the left there were refrigerators with glass doors so that we could see what was inside, they were filled with soft drinks. The first local looked at us with great confusion, but the second guy hopped to his feet and greeted us as he had known us for years. Trinity turned to me, "We came here the other night." Well it would have been nice to know that sooner, but for me the atmosphere was still very uneasy. The shopkeeper motioned for us to have a seat, the brothers moved in that direction so I followed suit. I was now finding out just what we were doing there. A few days prior the Herrington brothers had came to this shop and bought sodas for all of their guys, and they intended to do so again tonight.

The shopkeeper had disappeared to a back room and was now emerging with plates of steaming hot food. It looked like chicken and rice, it looked delicious. He sat the food on the table wanting us to eat it. I had to speak up "Guys, I don't think this is a good idea."

"Yeah, the big puss is probably right on this one," Trinity agreed to his brother. We insisted to the shopkeeper that we weren't hungry, but it was growing more tempting by the moment. It smelled really good and none of us had had hot food in weeks. Just as I was about to get up Brett said "Fuck it, you got to die of something," and threw a big handful of it in his mouth. Trinity and I were in shock, and sat for a minute fully expecting Brett to fall over dead. After a minute of convincing by Brett that it was "sooooo good" Trinity gave in and grabbed some. Shit!

"If I die or have the shits tomorrow, I'm gonna kick both of your asses," I said as I grabbed a handful. It was actually very good. We sat there and finished every bite of food there was on the huge plate, with the shopkeeper watching us eerily. When we finished the business began. Trinity and Brett each bought two cases of sodas to carry back and insisted I should as well.

"Oh yeah, and how do I explain where I got this, to my guys?" I asked sarcastically.

"Trust me you wont have too, no one will question it, and if they do just tell them you got it from us," Brett suggested. Damn that didn't sound like a half bad idea, and if I were to show up with Mountain Dew and Pepsis I would definitely be the hero. I decided to go for it and bought 24 sodas for $5. Not a bad deal ... if I don't get caught. We returned that night with the sodas and no trouble and it was just as the Herrington brothers had said it would be. Everyone was so happy for some caffeine that no one even questioned where it came from. I was hero of the moment!

The original plan for the Rangers called for us and a small group from the 82nd to jump into Baghdad International Airport. It was a very risky plan because no one was sure what Saddam was going to use against us. Once we landed we would be stuck on the ground for a long time in a relatively small area. If Saddam did use chemical agents on us the fall out could be tremendous. We did ROCK (practice for airfield seizure) drills for days preparing, and I continued to train up everyone on what to do should we face the unimaginable. People seemed to take me seriously now, but most were still skeptical that the equipment would work. Everyone in the company was sore at me because they had to carry chemical equipment in addition to their normal gear which was hella heavy. Three hours before go time, the entire plan was scrapped. A sigh of relief. Command was just too unsure what would happen and did not want a disaster to start off the war. The new plan called for Marines and 3rd ID to roll into the city. It was a good thing that they scrapped the plan because everyone was expecting at the most four or five tanks on the airfield. When the conventional Army arrived they found over sixty. It could have been a massacre.

Our new plan called for lots of new "toys". We were given Humvees for the first time ever, brand new Humvees, muhahaha. It didn't take long to start breaking things. The jeeps required a 500 mile break-in period, and we didn't have time for that. With the rough terrain 30 minutes after we began movement, we blew our first engine. I remember how nervous everyone was at the back of the convoy. We hadn't heard any explosions but we could see a raging fire coming from a vehicle at the front. There were dogs howling everywhere! Very uneasy!

We had moved across the Iraqi border and were taking ground very quickly. We had been going for about seventy-two hours and everyone needed some rest. We were in the desert and there wasn't much cover and concealment, so we would be vulnerable. But on the other hand we could see anyone coming at us for miles...right?

My vehicle had stopped and we all dismounted. The entire convoy seemed to have split up at this point and everyone was doing their own exploring. SSG Taylor, SPC Landers, and I plopped down our rucks and pulled out part of a MRE to eat. The XO and SPC Wilbanks continued to explore in the humvee. It was no time before all three of us had passed out.

"Wiggins! Landers! Wake up!" SSG Taylor seemed to scream in a whisper. He was laying in the prone and had his weapon at the ready which woke me up quick fast and in a hurry. Landers and I quickly followed suit. "Man I woke up and there was an Iraqi standing right over there about 100 meters." SSG Taylor anxiously pointed. Landers and I kept us covered while SSG Taylor tried to reach someone on the radio. The landscape was apparently flat and we should have been able to see for miles, but we couldn't spot any of our convoy. Not a good feeling. Had they forgotten us and left? Impossible, the Rangers would never leave a man behind, much less three. Still SSG Taylor couldn't get anyone on the radio and we couldn't see anyone.

"Alright here's what we are going to do. Landers gather all your shit and sprint to the berm over there Wiggins and I will cover you. When Landers gets there, Wiggins you go, and we will cover you. I'll bring up the rear and you two cover me." SSG Taylor instructed. We did so and then laid in the prone searching for something, anything, for hours. We never did see SSG Taylor's mystery man but about three hours later our jeep returned.

The XO pulled up asking "You guys get some good shut eye?" At which point SSG Taylor put his temper, which he was known for, into full effect. He not so subtly let the XO know that we only slept for 30 minutes and told him what happened. The XO being the ranking man in the group just laughed. "Well we have a perimeter set up so let's go over there and get cleaned up and then you can get some sleep," the XO ordered.

The next day Shock and Awe began. The air war. The war had finally started. Ha, what a joke. The planes on their way to Baghdad flew directly over us which I think was intentional and considered a morale booster. Everyone was definitely excited. We wouldn't get to see the campaign on T.V. till we got to Kuwait on our way back to the states.

With every town we would take we would gather thousands of A.K.-47's, and at most only a couple of prisoners. This night everything that could go wrong seemed to be going wrong for me. The route that we had chosen to take was extremely rough. Normally this wouldn't matter to me because I was a top gunner and that position is tough but you don't really get thrown to far. For this mission I was riding on the back of the Humvee. All my vehicle was assigned to do was support by fire. Basically when the assault force came in from the other side of town and people tried to escape out the back, we were there to make sure that didn't happen. We did so by shooting...a lot!

On the way to the town we kept hitting bumps. Not your average speed bumps. These "bumps" were like three and four foot berms. I was getting thrown all over the place. At one point my NODS hit the vehicle and somehow my batteries fell out. So while the Humvee was taking three foot berms, I was in the back trying to find my batteries with a red light. Of course everyone had their NODS on, so the red light was extremely bright and I was getting yelled at by everyone. Finally someone handed me an extra set of batteries they had. (Mental note: always carry extra batteries in your kit.)

I was in position and we were taking turns each firing a mag. into the town, mainly into the side of a pretty large building, just to scare the people from trying to run that way. After about ten minutes people started fleeing towards us even with us still shooting at them. Maybe in all the chaos they didn't realize where the bullets were coming from. They would finally start to realize where the bullets were coming from when they got halfway to us and then turn and run back in confusion. I was firing random shots mostly into the ground in front of people enticing them to return to where they came from. All except this one guy. I fired a couple of shots in front of him but

93

nothing was slowing him down. Wait, he is the only one wearing all white. What was it they told us about Iraqi's dressed in all white? Oh shit!! Suicide bomber! I took aim at his abdomen and carefully squeezed the trigger...nothing. Oh shit, oh shit, what a time for my piece of shit M4 to jam! I was performing SPORTS, which is a series of motions used to correct a jam (Slap, Pull, Observe, Release, Tap, Squeeze), on my weapon trying to un-jam it. The XO spotted the guy "Wiggins, take that guy down!" he ordered. "I'm on it sir," I assured him. Dumb, I should have told him my weapon was jammed so someone else could have taken the shot. But it was my shot and I wanted it. I could have gotten my entire group killed that night. Selfish! As the bolt finally rode forward and I pulled up and found the suspected terrorist in my NODS he was less than 20 meters away. I squeezed the trigger hoping for a reaction this time, and I got it. He went down. But one round from a M4 is probably not going to stop anyone unless it is a shot to the head. He was trying to get back up. As I fixed in for a head shot I was thinking, if this guy is a suicide bomber I wonder why there wasn't an explosion when the round hit him. But I don't get paid to think. The next round left him on the ground. Then I was given the "pleasure" of clearing the body. Guess what, no bomb. What in the hell was I suppose to do? I found out that night you can't question what happens in war, especially this kind of war. No matter how hard you try, you're going to be wrong some of the time.

It took about 24 hours to clear the entire town, and we had already been up an additional 24 at least. So when the town was cleared, we went out in the middle of no where for some rest. We set up a perimeter as always. Then I had the men set up the equipment that would detect a chemical attack another 100 meters outside the perimeter. This, in theory, would give us at least the eight seconds required to get on the pro-mask (gas-mask). We had been wearing the rest of the chemical suit the entire time in place of regular Dessert Combat Uniforms (DCU's). So if shit hit the fan, all we had to do was put on the mask. Unfortunately before we left the states, the entire company did not have time to qualify at the shooting range wearing the pro-mask. I worried about this on a daily basis.

I was cleaning my weapon inside of the perimeter when I looked onto the horizon and saw something strange. After watching it for about 30 seconds I could clearly tell whatever it is was headed straight for us. Assuming the worst I jumped up and threw my M4 in the Humvee and ran around screaming and pointing "GAS GAS GAS." Everyone immediately saw what I was pointing at and donned their pro-mask. Once everyone had their pro-mask on they started putting on their rubber boots and gloves, no one had much practice at this and they only we're half dressed when the "gas" arrived. It arrived in a force. The wind was easily blowing in excess of 100mph. No one could see anything. It was as though we were on Mars; everything looked red. I immediately reported to the Battalion Commander (BC) and intelligence officer. They were already working to find out what was going on.

A million things were running through my mind, all the scenarios that I had learned in NBC schools. This was crazy. I was taught how to tell if the gas had cleared, and it sucks. You find the lowest ranking man, someone not mission essential and you go through a series of removing the pro-mask. If he doesn't show symptoms in a certain amount of time you can give the all clear. Was I actually going to have to possibly kill one of my own Ranger buddies? No way! I had realized that the wind was still blowing really hard and that I couldn't explain. Then again I had never been in a chemical attack. I was remembering the movie *The Sum of All Fears*. I remembered how hard they had the wind blowing in the movie, but that was a nuclear attack. Oh shit a nuclear attack?! I'm being silly that was only in the movies. Who would nuke their own country?! Saddam Hussain that's who!! He had been notorious for doing stuff like this for years why not again, and to stop the world's only super power. That would be huge.

Wind storm in Iraq

Thank goodness it turned out to be a false alarm. It was "just" a wind storm. A wind storm that would last over 36 hours and halt all military operations. It was impossible to do anything. We couldn't see, couldn't breath, in a nut shell could not operate. I sincerely believe that this allowed plenty of time for hundreds of Iraqi soldiers to escape. If I were the enemy I would have used this opportunity to try some sort of counter attack. We heard that Iraqi civilians were interviewed to say that a wind storm like this only occurs when something very bad is about to happen. Maybe a silly notion, either way it's very interesting. It was noted that a wind storm of that magnitude and intensity had not been recorded anywhere in the Middle East, ever.

When the storm had passed, it took another day to get everything back in working order. All weapon systems had to be cleaned and tested. When I was done with my personal gear, I went to check out the chemical detection equipment. As I feared, everything was destroyed. None of the equipment would be any good to us any longer. We needed all new chemical equipment, I reported to the BC.

The BC stared off into space for a moment, "how much does all that equipment cost?"

"In the millions easily sir," I reported.

"Shit. Ok Wiggins, here is what is going to happen. You aren't going to tell anyone that the equipment doesn't work anymore. Got it?!" the BC ordered.

"Wait, what sir, I'm not sure I understand. You want the guys to lug around all of this equipment and not even tell them that it doesn't work?" I asked. "What if we are in a chemical attack?" The BC looked at me intensely.

"Wiggins, remember how mad everyone was at you that they had to carry this stuff in the first place?" I shook my head yes. "Well imagine how pissed they will be if they know they have to carry it and there is no way it may save their life. We cannot leave millions of dollars worth of military equipment out here." The BC argued.

Not knowing when to stop, I said "We could use C-4 and blow it sir." Again not the answer the BC wanted.

"Dammit, you have your orders Wiggins," the BC growled.

"Roger that, yes sir." I responded a little scared to argue anymore.

"On your way then." The BC ordered.

All I could think was that this is bullshit. I felt like I was totally screwing over my Ranger buddies. And what if there was a chemical attack. I would go down in history as the moron whose equipment was so jacked up that it got his entire unit killed. Once again I didn't like it, but as normal I was stuck between a rock and a hard place.

We continued to take village after village with little resistance. I personally blame it on the Unmanned Aerial Vehicle (U.A.V.). The Army had seen fit to give us these "high-speed" planes to fly over towns and see if there was any action there prior to our missions. Well first of all, we saw these as toys. Second they were so lightweight and the wind was always blowing so hard, it took us days to figure out how to keep one airborne. MSG Ferrusi was our top dog in intelligence and he pretty much out ranked everybody and he was frickin' huge, so he got to do all of the flying.

One day Ferrusi was trying to get this U.A.V. in the air and it went down behind a berm.

"What the fuck!" We all heard and assumed it had hit someone, so we were all laughing. Then 1st SGT Ardnts head popped up over the burm "Hey Ferrusi it's bad enough I gotta wipe my ass with sand paper over here, quit flyin planes into me!" He threw the plane back over the burm. Oh damn, Ferrusi had hit pretty much the only enlisted man that outranked him out here. We were all roaring with laughter. Anyway when we finally learned how to fly the plane well enough to get it into the town we were going to attack, we would always find literally hundreds of men walking around with rifles. Occasionally the U.A.V. would even get shot down. I mean come on, if you were an Iraqi soldier and you saw an American miniature airplane scoping out your town doesn't that tell you something is about to happen? So by the time we got to every town, no one would fight and all the men walking around sporting A.K.'s on surveillance was now a farmer. I've met many farmers by day and terrorists by night.

Finally we got a change of pace. We received orders to protect a huge dam. The U.S. was afraid Saddam would try to blow it and blame the U.S., which would turn the civilians against us. So our mission was to protect the dam until the conventional Army could get there and take over. We had been there for about two days when a character known as Baghdad Bob released a message on the radio and T.V. stating that we were going to destroy the dam. For some reason the Iraqi people believed this. And just like that, gravy duty was over. Iraqi civilians started coming out of the woodwork to try to drive us off the dam. At least most of the Iraqi's played it smart and came out to protest unarmed. No one wants to shoot a civilian, but there were some cases where we didn't have a choice. It was very unsafe conditions for everyone and some people were very angry. They were yelling and firing their weapons into the air. It was a very uneasy atmosphere. After the first civilian was knocked down, the crowd became even more enraged. It was growing out of hand fast. Finally 3rd ID got there and used their loud speakers and interpreters to dispel the rumor that we were going to cause any damage to the dam and the crowd began to disperse. It's funny what people will do just because they are told.

Tigris River in Iraq

Well the regular Army had taken over the dam and we were waiting on orders. Rangers tend to get restless real fast. It had been just over a month since anyone had seen running water. We were all caked in dirt and mud and reeked to high heaven. Here we were sitting beside this beautiful river. It was the Tigris River and it was amazing and inviting. Before I knew it there were about 30 naked Rangers playing in the water. Keep in mind that on the dam there were females in the 3rd ID unit, not that any of us cared. After maybe ten minutes at most our commander came outside and found what was going on.

"What in the hell are you Rangers doing?" Everyone froze "This is the Tigris River, don't you know that there are piranhas in there?" the commander said, half laughing half serious. I don't know to this day if that was true, but it was a sight seeing 30 naked Rangers hauling ass out of that river.

Time to move out. We had a mission to go occupy a terrorist training camp. I had no idea of the things I would see there. When they told us terrorist training camp, I assumed it would just be a town that they had labeled that. It in fact had the works. Obstacle courses, thousands upon thousands of A.K.-47s, and even chemical protection equipment, everything you could imagine. There were several operational motorcycles and even a couple of tanks. I will admit I shed a tear when the Army had us lay out the thousands of A.K.-47's and then ran a tank over them. Some ranger managed to salvage one and taped it to the bottom of a Humvee hoping to sneak it back into the States but customs found it.

We were running missions out of this compound for about a week and everything was going smoothly. Then one night we were on a recon mission and we took incoming. We thought it was a mortar and it destroyed the entire jeep, killing Rangers and Delta Force personnel. We quickly learned that the incoming came from a 3rd ID tank. The tank thought that we were the enemy. How in the hell?! We had all of our vehicles marked with IR (infer red) and glint tape specifically so this wouldn't happen. The excuse the tank made was that it was too dark to see any of that and the tank just picked us up with the heat sensors. It was all a bunch of bullshit. Mistakes like that should not happen with the U.S. military. We held a memorial for the guys killed in action (K.I.A.) the next day then began working on a solution so we wouldn't get hit by anymore tanks. We had heat shields on the way but it would be a couple of weeks before they arrived. The heat shields merely hung on the side of the jeep showing tankers that we were not the enemy. So what we came up with in the mean time was MRE heater bags. The heater bags have chemicals in them that when you add water to them they heat up. They stay hot for a very long time which worked perfectly.

Wild dogs had taken over this compound. Most were not aggressive just aggravating. They whimpered, whined, and barked all day and all night, hundreds of them. Some guys simply couldn't sleep with all the noise. The order was out that we were not to harm the dogs.

Some Ranger's like to carry hatchets with their gear. It really serves no purpose but is a long standing tradition that dates all the way back to Rogers Rangers in the Revolutionary War. This is where you can date the concept of the Ranger as officially being founded. These Rangers would hide out and move through the swamps and unconventionally assault enemy troops, as opposed to the tradition of lining up and shooting at one another. Back then there was a sense that war could be civilized and many times the ranking officers would even offer the first shot to the other side. War is never civilized! Any way these first Rangers would move through the thick forest and their hatchets came in quite handy for getting through tight spots, and of course became instrumental in close combat.

So in modern day Iraq was this Ranger trying to get to sleep, with his hatchet, after putting up with yelping dogs for over a week. Sgt. Peter's had just completed PLDC, which is the leadership school one must attend to retain the rank of sergeant. He literally returned to base and got right on the plane for Iraq. Many were shocked that the Rangers were retaining him because he was known for taking things to far. One time he came into the barracks drunk and stuck a loaded hand gun into a private's mouth while he smoked him. This information had made its rounds but was never taken to higher and therefore he was never reprimanded for it. Night after night he would scream obscenities at these dogs, which was almost more annoying than the dogs. One night he finally snapped, reached over grabbed his hatchet and flung it in the general direction of the barking dogs. Suddenly the yelping stopped. There was a short cheer followed by a whimpering. The hatchet had caught the puppy right in the stomach and was stuck in him. Suddenly everyone felt bad.

Sgt. Peter's platoon sergeant already didn't like him and used this as an excuse to try and take him down. Sgt. Peters was assigned to burning shit the rest of the deployment and the rest of his punishment would take place when we returned stateside. It was decided that Sgt. Peters would undergo evaluation when we returned home and during this time he would be removed from the line. He made it through these trying times and went on to get his E-6 in the Rangers. I don't believe Peters was all right upstairs, but he was one of the damn finest Rangers I ever met. He wound up finally being RFS'd from battalion for being caught leaving a CIA compound stateside to Iraq with a shampoo bottle full of liquor. Someone who had it out for him had a general recommend his removal. He would later find his way back into Special Forces.

We had moved on from the terrorist compound and were nomads again. It had been an extremely long day, I'd say about 72 hours, when we reached our link up point. The order to get some shut eye never sounded so good. We downloaded our gear and all racked out leaning against our rucks. I woke up several times because it was daytime and very bright and hot, but easily fell back to sleep because I was so tired. My platoon sergeant woke me up, a little too late, just as it was with the rest of the company. We were sunburnt, bad.

I will never forget the first time I heard it; it was like something out of the movies. "We are going to rescue a P.O.W. from behind enemy lines." Ah I get it this is a joke, its April Fools day after all. But supposedly no one was joking. A little history for my readers. The last successful P.O.W. rescue from

105

behind enemy lines occurred in WWII. The mission is known as The Great Raid. The P.O.W.'s were survivors from the Batton Death March. The rescuers: Airborne Rangers of course.

As the story unfolded, it seemed that the Marines had been trying to take this city for three days but got pushed out every time. Intense!! As it turned out a young soldier, a WOMAN, had been captured by the Iraqi's. Her supply truck had gotten separated from the rest of the convoy, and they got lost. Nine U.S. Army soldiers were missing but we only had information on one. Private Jessica Lynch. An Iraqi doctor had approached the fence around our compound under a white flag. It was a miracle that he wasn't shot. He told the command that there was a U.S. soldier in his hospital under the name Private Jessica Lynch. What was he getting out of telling us this valuable information? Why a first class ticket to the U.S. of course. He said that he could not return to the city because there Iraqi soldiers were watching our compound and he would be killed. If the information he gave us was true it certainly deserved a U.S. citizenship. This doctor told us that Private Lynch was in pretty bad shape, and we needed to get to her as soon as possible. Sound like an ambush to you?

We started to plan for the mission that was to take place that night. The plan was conjuring up bad memories for many Rangers. This was a city with millions of Iraqis in it. The mission was to occur at night, but we were to drive out of the city in broad day light. We have a saying in the Army. Always expect the worst, but hope for the best. This mission reminded lots of rangers of 1993 in

Mogadishu, Somalia where 18 servicemen were killed when the operation went horribly wrong. Rangers began nicknaming the mission Mogadishu 2 and Operation Send My Son to Harvard. It just didn't seem like a good plan. Higher even decided that the GO command would be the same command was used in Somalia a decade earlier; IRENE.

We found ourselves loading up onto trucks that night with Navy Seals. A company from 2nd Battalion would chopper in a few blocks away in an attempt to draw as much enemy fire as possible towards them. As we were entering the city, it was amazing. Every Ranger on the convoy must have been scanning with their laser which can only be seen through NODS. To the Iraqi soldier it was just a dark night, but what I was seeing was the most amazing light show ever. The entire sector of that city was lit up. The Iraqi's could hear us coming and were moving around unaware that we could see their every move. The choppers carrying Bco. (Bravo Company) from 2nd Battalion must have landed at that exact moment because I was startled by sporadic gun fire. One Ranger, a private, said "hooah." Following suit as SEALs always seem to do, one of the SEALs made fun of the Ranger for saying hooah. The Navy SEALs had already let me down twice, but I don't believe it talking badly about any of our Uniformed Services. The remark was unappreciated.

Just as we entered the city, there was an accident with the vehicle ahead of us. The ammo for the top gun had come loose and fell onto the driver's head knocking him unconscious and causing the vehicle to run into a building. Another ranger who was sitting on the back of the vehicle was resting his Ranger Body Armor (RBA) on the railing of the vehicle and broke his back. It was decided that three or four Rangers would stay with the "wounded" and the rest of us would carry on, on foot. This wasn't as bad as it seemed as the hospital was only about two blocks away and I'd rather be on foot in these circumstances than in a vehicle anyway. But I must admit I had flashes of the movie *Black Hawk Down* running through my head.

As we turned the corner to the hospital, the same Navy SEAL that had laughed at my Ranger buddy called the group to a halt. He then eased around the corner to shoot out the light. A whisper of air swished as he fired his decked out weapon with the silencer on it. Hmmm, I still see light. The SEAL stepped back around the corner and looked at his weapon strangely. "Wind must have picked up." I was amused. The SEAL scoffed and turned back around the corner to take another shot. Swish...still nothing. The SEAL seemed annoyed and was looking over his weapon when I instructed "Private Hooah" to take the shot. "BAM!!" the shot rang out followed by the light exploding. I just gave the SEAL a smartass look and went back to work.

Our job was to secure the outside of the hospital while the medics and big brass went inside to retrieve Private Lynch. We were taking minimal small arms fire, not nearly what we expected and we were glad. Suddenly SGT Barrio screamed "Wiggins get your K-Pot on!" What in the hell was he talking about? I had my Mitch (modified Kevlar) on. At that second it must have hit him that we don't wear Kevlars and he moved over to inspect it. Oh shit it had blood on it. We both searched for someone missing a helmet but everyone seemed squared away. Just then we realized we were taking a knee on a mound of freshly placed dirt. Both of us must have had the same thought at the same time because we both looked at each other and said "No!" Only one way to find out. One of us would take turns covering the other while one used the butt stock of his M4 and hands to dig. Sure enough after about three feet of digging we discovered a black American soldier. There were seven other mounds just like this so we got into buddy teams and began digging. In the meantime SGT Barrio relayed our findings to the commander "Sir we found the rest of the missing soldiers, they're buried in front of the hospital. We are digging them up." Seemingly not shocked at all the commander said he would inform the pick up chopper to bring body bags.

As we had just finished unearthing all of the bodies, Rangers started to emerge from the hospital. Just then a medic chopper landed and they brought Private Lynch out on a stretcher and put her on the chopper. The only view I got of Private Lynch was of her kicking and screaming and fighting everyone that was trying to help her. I understand being scared, but wow. The sun was just coming up as we set to depart. Now for the hard part, getting out alive.

As the convoy took off and we rounded the first corner, people started flocking to the streets. Oh crap, here we go. What is this?! They were all waving American flags and seemed very happy for our success. Not at all what we expected, and we remained very alert till we were completely out of the city. When we crossed the last bridge out of the city, we began to realize what we had just accomplished. The high fives began. We didn't understand, however, why the Marines hadn't been able to take the city. The only scenario that we could come up with is that they saw the force that was coming and hauled ass. We did have special weaponry that the conventional military did not have. I would have run too!

"Ok men, good job on the Lynch rescue but we aren't finished yet. Our next mission is to jump into HLZ1," our commander briefed us. Wait, did he just say jump? Why were we jumping? We had just been making fun of the 173rd, a new airborne unit out of Italy for getting a mustard stain with no kills. At this point in the war no Iraqi was really standing up and fighting and none of us wanted to go through the bullshit of a "combat jump." Nevertheless parts of the 75th did jump and just as we thought there was no one on the ground. When I arrived I had nothing in my ruck so that when we landed I cut the 550 cord and stuffed a chute in my ruck. There were parachuted flying in the desert wind the entire time we were there. No one took it upon themselves to collect them. We set up shop at HLZ1 and stayed there for about two weeks. I still have mine to this day in my basement.

One day it rained and once again there were dozens of Rangers butt naked running around. It was really starting to become a serious health issue at this point because lets face it, we were at war and Rangers were running around with Iraqi's blood on their uniforms. Really starting to stink.

One day the commander announced that there

110

was a volunteer mission if anyone wanted it. What do you learn day one in the Army? Never volunteer for anything. But I was tired of burning shit, literally burning shit. When you are in one place for a while, that's what you do. Everyone shits into barrels and twice a day it has to be burned. Yes it is as nasty as it sounds.

About ten of us volunteered, for guess what? Escort duty! We were to protect this group of 3rd ID tankers who were assigned to go to the Syrian border and make sure that no one was crossing. Are you kidding me?! A unit of the U.S. Army should not need to be protected. But here we were looking at a mountain range in the far distance.

Then the Air Force showed up and gave us a bit of a show. Intelligence was that there was an underground missile factory there and the Air Force was bombing the hell out of it. Every day for about a week they would swing through the neighborhood and drop a few bombs on it and that would be our show for the day. Then one day we were watching our firework show and two bombs came down then suddenly there was one coming back up, then it leveled out heading straight for us. Someone yelled "incoming" but it was like ok, where are we gonna go? All we could do was get low and hope for the best. Well, we lucked out and got the best. The missile slammed into the earth about a mile short of us causing no damage. I guess the Air Force finally hit their underground missile factory. The daily fireworks show ceased.

Air Force workin' in Iraq

One day I was pulling my guard shift on a .50 cal that was fastened to the top of one of the tanks. It was in shitty condition and not well maintained and everything was loose. The order was when people reached a certain point, we were to fire warning shots and if they approached any further call it in. There were two signs of warning about 100 meters before they reached a point that we had to fire warning shots. Even so, every day we would have to fire warning shots several times. This day was no different. I had already fired warning shots myself three different times. My guard shift was about over when a family wandered past the signs and was coming up on the warning shots mark. I fired warning shots, and of course the family hit the ground. You had to be really careful because the mount on the gun was so loose and it had such a kick. When the family got back to their feet I expected them to turn around and head the other direction, but they didn't, they continued straight for us. They didn't even have a white flag. This was dumb I thought. So I followed procedure and asked higher what they wanted me to do. I was instructed to fire more warning shots. Roger that, I love the .50 cal. So I fired another burst of warning shots. Once again the family hit the ground. About a minute later the family was on their feet and running in the opposite direction. I was chuckling to myself for a second when I realized there were only three people running. Where in the hell did the forth guy go. I was scanning the sector for movement but there was none. Of course others noticed what had been happening too.

"Wiggins where did you fire?" the 1st SGT from the 3rd ID unit asked.

"About 60 meters in front the approaching suspects Top" I responded. Evidently Top is what a lot of units call their 1st SGT.

"Well keep an eye out there. Make sure this guy doesn't pop up on us." Five minutes and still nothing. By now the rumor had spread all over that I had shot some guy that approached the fence. I knew this wasn't true I didn't even aim near him, but something was definitely up. Finally, Higher decided to send a three man team out to check it out. When they reported back I was shocked. The guys head had been ripped almost completely off. There was no sign that a bullet ever hit him though. It was finally concluded that the warning shot that I fired must have ricocheted off a rock and the sheer velocity of the round going by his head killed him. I felt bad. I had already learned that shit happens in war, but I still felt bad.

Finally we got to return to our guys and, of course, everyone was joking that I couldn't shoot.

But the guys back at the compound had some excitement while we were gone too. A fighter jet had somehow been shot down and my guys were sent to look for the pilot. They easily found the wreckage and absolutely nothing was salvageable. It didn't take long to find the pilot either, or should I say parts of him. So while they were bringing what they could find of this pilot back to the compound, a pick-up truck came hauling ass up on the convoy. The rear gunner fired warning shots at the vehicle but he didn't slow down any. The truck ended up with a windshield full of .50 cal. When the convoy stopped to check it out it looked as though it was just a fisherman who was in a bit too much of a hurry.

EX-Dictator of Iraq, Saddam Hussain

It had been a long three months when we heard that we were going home. It did seem to go by fast because we were always so busy, but everyone was excited to get home. We took a Chinook to Kuwait where we would catch a plane home. The fly boys were showing off I guess, doing all kinds of crazy maneuvers. I thought "Great, I survived Iraq to be killed in a helicopter crash." It seemed like there had been a helicopter crash once a week and now I see why. We had done several operations strapped to the sides of little birds which are small helicopters. You strap to the sides of them and they move across the land at very low altitudes at about 130mph. It wasn't frightening for me, but these guys were just being reckless.

We made it to Kuwait and we had 12 hours till our flight. The first thing everyone did was head to the chow hall. This was the first hot meal any of us had had in three months. I was sitting there eating when this soldier who was deployed to Kuwait started complaining that his ice cream was melted, if you can believe. I chose to ignore him, but I wanted to give him a piece of my mind.

Being that we were the first group to leave Iraq, Delta Airlines donated a flight home to us. The pilots and attendants were all very kind to us, even after we made a few of them puke because of our smell. The commander had put out an order that we were to all keep our boots on, good idea. When we were off the ground, as is tradition, we sang the Star Spangled Banner. I saw a couple of the attendants crying. I'll admit I got a bit misty eyed myself. It was an awesome flight home. They showed us several movies and we had all you can eat. Anytime that we wanted more food they brought it to us, no questions asked. I swear I ate the entire flight. We also were allowed to use the air-phones at no charge to us. This was really nice because we were not allowed any contact with our familis for the last 3.5 months. I wasn't wasting my phone call to Lola this time. I called my grandma who was very surprised and happy to hear from me. We were not allowed to tell our family when we would be home, but I did tell my grandma I was calling from a plane at 40,000 feet. I'm pretty sure that she got the picture. The pilots were also letting us take turns "flying" the plane. Basically they were just allowing us to sit at the controls. We were getting ready for our final approach into Rome when I got my turn to fly. It was amazing!

As I was unpacking and cleaning my gear, all I could find on T.V. was Jessica Lynch this and Jessica Lynch that. It had been more than a few weeks since the rescue occurred, but it was still a hot story evidently. As it turned out the media had made Private Lynch into a war hero and she was getting a million dollar book deal and a free ticket out of the military. What in the hell is really going on?! Let's review shall we? She got lost, was involved in an ambush in which she didn't fire a shot, all of her comrades were killed and she was taken hostage. When being rescued, she kicked and screamed the entire way. I don't want to say anything bad about her, what she went through was very intense I'm sure. But do you think that we ever even got a thank you from Private Lynch? Nope. Later we heard that there was going to be a T.V. movie made about her experience. We decided it would be fun to send the T.V. station our real names and who we wanted to play our part in the movie. The suggestions ranged from Nicholas Cage to Steven Segal. I guess her story wasn't that big after all because they couldn't get one of those actors to star in it.

I want to share a story with you about a real hero. This story takes place back in Dessert Storm. There was a Spec. Ops. Mission and when the mission was nearing an end and when the helicopters came to pick the men up, one of the helicopters fell off of the side of the building it had landed on. All of the other helicopters and men had already taken off and everyone inside of this helicopter was killed except one Delta Force guy. When the rest of the group realized what had happened, they of course returned to the scene of the incident. When they arrived, a heated battle erupted and during the chaos, they found the severely injured soldier lying in the open. The soldiers rushed to him and formed a shield around him making sure he didn't get injured any more than he already had been. They were taking intense fire and the Delta guy told them that he didn't need to be babied and to give him a fire arm because he was still in the fight. They did give him that fire arm and he was instrumental in their escape. That's a hero! Do you think anyone ever heard this story or that he got a million dollar book deal or a T.V. movie? Nope! But I know his type and I know that he is ok with that. Hell, he is probably still serving in some elite top secret unit out there somewhere.

It's funny because after people learned that we were home, everyone wanted to thank us. I found this odd. One day I was walking out of Wal-Mart when this lady stopped me.

"Are you a Ranger?" she asked.

"Yes I am" I said proudly.

"Well I just wanted to tell you how proud my family is of you and thank you for serving in Iraq."

She hugged me.

"Ma'am I didn't go to Iraq for you, I went for the Iraqi people. If you want to thank us, thank us for going to Afghanistan." I informed her. She looked at me as though she had never heard of Afghanistan. What a shame.

O.E.F. 4

After an eight month break from war we were getting ready to head back. This time we were heading to Afghanistan. Everyone was excited. Why? Because we "knew" where Bin Laden is!! This was it. This was the whole reason I joined the military, to get this asshole. We had confirmed intelligence that he was up high in the mountains in a town called Khoust. There was no way the military was going to risk him getting away this time. They were calling in the best. Word was he was waiting out winter there before he moved. This would mean hell for the Rangers, but the prize at the end was so sweet who cared. We were out of the states within 48 hours of receiving this intel.

The Army had given us all new gear including Oakley boots and sunglasses. Well Christmas was coming up and we would deserve it after this mission. After driving for three or four days from Baghram Air Field, we finally reached a small compound that Delta had already established. The briefing was terrifying. It was impossible to drive any further; we would have to go on foot the rest of the way up. This was about 20,000 feet up in the mountains and it was all snow. I was one of the tallest Rangers in the group and at the time and the snow was hip deep on me. It was very slow going and almost impossible to sleep at night. The Army had issued us cold weather gear, but it felt like none of it worked after the first night our core temperatures dropped very low and they never got back up. Some Rangers got so sick they lost up to 30 lbs. in less than a week. It could have been from sleeping in sub-zero temperatures without any shelter what-so-ever or some guys found a little shed and opted to sleep inside…in donkey shit.

The Khoust region of Afghanistan

Finally the day came that we would reach the area where all of the terrorists supposedly were, and we were expecting a pretty good fight, so everyone was checking and re-checking their gear. We sent out three recon teams at around midnight to monitor our movement and hopefully catch us if we were walking into a trap. We hadn't seen anyone the entire walk, but they always somehow knew when we were coming.

We had the town in sight when two shots rang out above us. The recon team came in handy. There were two Al-Queda lookouts waiting to snipe us from a seemingly un-climbable hill. But it was climbable and within a couple of hours a team of Rangers returned with their report. There was a cave up there with hundreds of uniforms and weapons and other military paraphernalia. Wow, this was actually it.

We moved in and began clearing the town. Like always we confiscated quite a few weapons, but where the hell were the terrorist? Many town folk told us that Osama had in fact been there but had left just a day or two before. They had no idea who we were or why we were looking for him. That was their story anyway, and they all seemed to be together on it and sticking to it. Another huge disappointment, but it was obvious we were disrupting things for Al-Queda and that was very encouraging.

We stayed on the move clearing town after town. Finally I guess we found "the spot" and we set up a compound to run missions out of. The townsfolk came out and just stood and watched us...for days. It didn't seem like they slept or ate or anything, they just stood there and watched, hundreds of them.

We quickly found out that no opposing force had been up there since Alexander the Great, and these people had no idea what was going on. Most of them had never heard of Osama Bin Ladin and absolutely no one had any knowledge of 9/11. Our officers had a meeting with the town elders and briefed them on what was going on, assuring them that we were not there to hurt them. Then the daily mortars began.

Daily I would hear "incoming" followed by a screaming mortar. If you have never heard a mortar incoming it makes a very loud, very unsettling whistling. What makes the feeling worse than being in a fire fight? Well the simple question, where do you run for cover? There is no way to tell where that mortar is going to hit till it hits and that's a bad feeling. Luckily, the enemy, in this case, usually set up launchers on sticks and is long gone before the round is ever fired. This means the aim is usually way off. I don't think out of the dozens of incoming mortar rounds we took that month that one got closer than a couple hundred yards away. We always figured our luck would run out one day though.

One day we were coming back from a mission and I noticed the cutest little girl watching us and walking a ways behind us but following us nonetheless. This happened a lot out of sheer interest, and I had attached a stuffed animal to my .50 cal and when you squeezed its paw it humped the gun and barked; the kids loved it.

I was getting very complacent and thinking to myself you know, these are some beautiful people if you could get them out of the country in time before it takes its toll on them as it does to everyone. Most Afghan women are very beautiful up to the age of maybe 15, then the country starts to wear on them and it gets bad. We had just exited the town and the little girl had stopped at the edge. Suddenly I hard a loud explosion and thought to myself the same thing everyone else was thinking, ah the daily mortar attack. I looked behind me again and much to my surprise, I saw a huge cloud of smoke and a flaming Hilux pick-up truck at the edge of town.

"Holy Shit Sergeant, look" I yelled. SSG Taylor picked up the double time to the rear where he met me.

"What happened Wiggins? Was it a mortar?" he asked.

"I'm not sure sergeant. I didn't hear any whistle did you?" I answered. No one else had heard a mortar incoming either, and we set out to investigate the vehicle. Slowly and carefully approaching the vehicle it was obvious that the driver was dead. It suddenly occurred to me, where is the little girl? I reminded SSG Taylor of her and he sent another Ranger and me to search for her. We first searched in the immediate area with no luck, then searched around town no luck either. I pray to God she just ran off somewhere, but we never found her.

We quickly found that what had caused the explosion was an Improvised Explosive Device (IED). You hear of these being used all the time in Afghanistan and Iraq. When we questioned the town if they knew anything about it, everyone seemed to know. They told us that it was not meant for us but rather a local border patrolman. Playing police officer, we demanded to know who set it up. We were told to mind our own business. I thought this is bullshit. Anytime someone gets robbed they come running to us for justice, but now they don't want us to play cop anymore.

It was Thanksgiving Day 2003, and the Army had seen fit to fly us out some "real food," and the Rangers had seen fit not to give us any missions that day; God bless them all. We were all excited to be getting some hot grub, and although we still knew it would be terrible, we had learned tricks to fix it up some. As we sat down to our makeshift tables so that the officers could serve us as is tradition, they started slopping food on our plates and we found that all of the food had ice in it. Everyone just kind of looked at one another then started laughing. There was no way we were going to eat this shit. A few Rangers got up to get MRE's. "Every Ranger will eat every bit of food that is on his plate." The highest ranking NCO shouted. Shit, I knew this good day would get ruined somehow. So we sat there and ate our cold peas with so much to be thankful for.

Yum Army cookin'...with ice!!!

After our bountiful feast everyone split up. We had no task to do, so it was fuck off time. Some Rangers spent it with their Gameboy Advances, some with their MP3s, and some of us played Spades, which is a favorite pastime on a Ranger deployment. Then out of nowhere one ranger yelled "Hey, who wants to play football?" Everyone quickly looked to him like he was the biggest retard on earth "Where are you gonna get this football?" He held up a crazy contraption and then whipped it to another Ranger. It threw pretty good. He had taken a water bottle and wrapped, and wrapped, and wrapped it with 100 MPH (Duct) tape. So there we were, 15 Rangers playing Thanksgiving Day football in the middle of a combat zone. It was intense. It should have been televised, I think.

Every year when we are in the States for Thanksgiving, we have a Turkey Bowl in which the officers play the enlisted. Needless to say the enlisted guys always win. (My story, I will tell it how I want.) One year some of the Jacksonville Jaguars who are located right down the road from our base came up and scrimmaged with us. I wont put anyone down, but I think we surprised them big time.

2003 Turkey Bowl in The Ghan

Our compound was located high up in the mountains, but in a valley nonetheless. The terrain in between all of the villages we had to clear was relatively flat, so the Army kindly sling loaded us a few Gun Mounted Vehicles (GMV's). This was a risky move because the Chinooks would have to fly in between a lot of mountains slinging the GMV's all over the place and could easily place a Chinook in the side of a mountain. The Army had also, by this point, seen fit to fly out a 10th Mountain group and a Marine group to us to pull guard on our compound so that we could concentrate solely on missions. So we now had GMV's which meant a lot less walking. This also meant I was back on top gunner detail.

GMV being Sling-loaded in

One night we were clearing this huge village that was spread out on both sides of a river. There was only one rope bridge which made maneuvering very difficult. I was assigned to sit on

128

top of the hill on the .50 cal and keep eye on the boys through my heat sensor scope and night vision. Normally this would be the job anyone would want. For some reason this night it wasn't snowing, it was raining, a freezing rain and I didn't bring any gortex. I sat soaked and freezing for over 6 hours before they were done clearing that town. I was shaking so bad I could not have shot anything at that point anyways.

That night when we returned to the compound, I decided to sleep in the tent. I had refused up to this point, even though it was freezing outside, due to the fact that it was one huge green tent on the side of the mountain. If I were wanting to kill the enemy I would probably aim at their big green tent on the side of a mountain, so I chose to sleep a few hundred yards away. A couple of other Rangers joined me. When I got into the tent I immediately stripped down in front of everybody and located my bear suit, which had been issued to us in case of extremely cold weather; this qualified. I got into my sleeping bag still shaking uncontrollably trying to get my core temperature to rise. Though it had been a few hours and I had been sleeping, it seemed like no time at all before my guard shift arrived. "Wiggins wake up it's your guard shift." Ranger Anderson whispered. He started shaking me. I DID NOT want to leave that sleeping bag. Finally I muttered "Fuck you." He took this as I was up and would be there shortly which is exactly what I meant. We'll call it Ranger talk. I reached over for my DCU's. Aw man, they are still soaked and freezing! I thought to myself there is no way I'm putting on my gear. I grabbed my weapon and headed for the gate. We had to guard the front gate because evidently Marines and 10th Mountain are

129

not competent enough to do so. I approached to relieve the Ranger for duty "Fuck you man, you can't pull guard in that shit." I had none of my gear only my bear suit, my weapon and night vision. I just plopped down on the sandbags and didn't say a word. He picked up quickly on not to screw with me that night, good choice.

Every morning every Ranger must be up and standing by for what is known as "stand to" when we are forward (not at a secured base.) I am normally a very friendly morning person but after the night I had just had I wasn't in the mood for any bulshit today. Just as I walked out of the tent I saw a private climbing into my gun turret.

"What is the hell do you think you're doing Ranger?" I asked irritated. Going anywhere near a top gunners weapon, except when pulling guard, is highly unacceptable.

"Just tryin' to get as close to the sun as possible and warm up specialist," the Ranger replied in desperation.

"Ha, you're a jackass. You think three feet is gonna help. You know the sun is like a gazillion miles away right?!" I informed him sarcastically.

"No it's not specialist," pointing at the sun "It's right there!" At first I assumed he was being a smart ass and was just about to lay into him when I noticed a look of sincerity on his face. I didn't even feel like dealing with his ignorance but wow.

A few days later we were out clearing another town, routine deal. Then we came across something interesting. A man in the town by the name Muhammad YaYa was found with a butt load of cash on him, way more than the rest of the town had all together. He was a well dressed and well spoken gentleman and even spoke English very well. Muhammad YaYa had knowledge of everything. Anything we asked him about he knew. He had to be Al-Queda, and high up. After weeks of searching towns and picking up multiple suspects, we had finally found the real thing, for sure. We got him back to the compound and were told we would have to keep him for a few days till the next bird came out and they would take him back to BAF (Baghram Air Field) for interrogation. While he was there he didn't get tortured, but he definitely was not being treated very good. All Enemy Prisoners of War (EPW's) were to remain tied up and have a sand bag over their heads at all times. The orders were to just watch him and give him food and water every once in a while, just enough to survive of course. His piss hole was about 3 feet from him.

One ranger who volunteered constantly to pull guard on him was Ranger Anderson. Ranger Anderson was actually a Ranger Cook, and cooks don't get to go out very much, but due to the fact that we were spread so thin he had gotten to tag along to the compound. He didn't ever really get to go out on the missions with us, which irked him visibly, but he was happy to be out at all after spending the last two deployments at BAF. This was his first time getting his hands on the enemy and he was taking as much advantage of it as he could. I remember every time I would walk by Muhammad YaYa, Anderson would be sitting there throwing skittles at the sand bag over his face. When I'd ask Anderson what he was doing he just replied, "eh, it's not hurting him."

Finally the bird came and took the EPW to BAF. A few days later Muhammad YaYa returned. As it turned out, he checked out. He was the head

131

school master for the entire region and all the money he had was a collection to buy school materials. The day after Muhammad YaYa was returned, I noticed he was still walking around the compound, with guards of course.

"Hey, why is that guy still here? Isn't anyone gonna take him home?" I asked.

The ranking man said "Yeah, we are taking him to his home in the morning. We were going to take him last night but he insisted that he would like to stay and serve everyone dinner tonight to show that there is no hard feelings." Holy shit, are you serious? On that day I stopped hating all Afghans. Muhammad YaYa was a great man.

That night as Ranger Anderson and I laid there looking up at the stars bullshitting, suddenly Anderson said "Hey see that bright star?"

"Yeah" I replied.

"That star is Muhammad YaYa's. I laughed but Anderson didn't. Every night for the rest of our stay there before we would go to sleep either Anderson or myself would look up at that star post a long sigggghhhh followed by goodnight Muhammad YaYa. It really bothered Anderson how he treated Muhammad YaYa only to find out what a good guy he was. That's war, Ranger Anderson.

About a week out from Christmas we got word that the Marines and 10th Mountain were returning to BAF for Christmas. What in the hell is that?! Why do they get to go?! Then on the day they were supposed to leave, the Chinook that had come to pick them up had gotten about 50feet in the air and dropped like a rock severely injuring everyone on board. The Seargent Major who was out there with 10th Mountain was doing Hail

Mary's. You see this helicopter ride would be his last. He had served 32 years and when he got home this time, he would be staying for good. They got another Chinook out the next day to pick up 10th Mountain. Something happened to that chopper on the way home and it never made it. Everyone on board was killed. I don't really feel bad for the rest of the soldiers because it's war and these things happen. But that SMG not making it home really hit me hard. It wasn't fair; he had served his country well, his time was up all he had to do was get home.

December 23, 2003 is a day I will never forget. We were on a ground movement, meaning we were walking. We had been walking and walking for hours when finally we came to the last mountain that we had to go around to reach the link-up point. The movement consisted of 3rd platoon and four attachments, which included SSG Taylor, myself, and two recce (recon) guys. The recce guys had scouted out the route the last couple of days and were pretty much leading the way. We reached a point and one recce Ranger told the platoon leader "This is where we go up sir."

"What in the hell are you talking about that's not what I have on the map, the trail leads all the way around the base of the mountain." Said Lt. Meyers.

"Yes sir, but instead of walking all the way around the mountain if you cross over here it will save you about ten hours." informed recce.

Looking up the Lt. pondered the climb. "It's to steep, some of these guys are carrying over a hundred pounds of equipment. There's no way we can make it up," ordered the Lt.

"Sir, we are both carrying over 100lbs of
133

equipment and we both made it yesterday. Yes it's a bitch but these guys are Rangers sir, they can handle it," argued recce.

"We aren't attempting it and that's final," ordered the Lt.

"That's fine" recce said "but we aren't walking all the way around this mountain, we will meet you there," spouted off recce, which was crazy because he was basically telling an officer what he was going to do.

"I don't give a fuck what you do." Shouted the Lt.

SSG Taylor then chimed in "Sir, if it's ok with you, Wiggins and I will stick with recce." It was agreed the four of us would meet the rest of the platoon on the other side. Looking almost straight up thousands of feet I turned to SSG Taylor and asked "What have you got us into sergeant?" He just chuckled and assured me we would be fine.

Recce led the way up and it was slow going I was wearing well over 85lbs of equipment. Every step I made was an unsure one and what kept me motivated was looking back. There was nothing for almost a thousand feet, and then there was the ground which consisted of huge boulders.

¼ way up "The Climb" (approx. 500ft.)

The air was so thin I could hardly breath! I took a step and slipped, a bunch of little rocks went flying. I watched them fall to the ground. I was almost there now with maybe 150 feet to go, but I was running out of fuel quickly. Somehow we all made it to the top and there was a one lane dirt road there which we all laid in for about 30 minutes. Finally recovering somewhat it was time to move out. We started walking down the dirt path and had gone about one mile when out of nowhere a Hilux truck pulled up. We scrounged between us and came up with $50 for the driver to drive us to the link up point. I remember thinking to myself…wow that was nice, wonder why we didn't just force him to take us? Thirty minutes later we were there. I slept for about 7 or 8 hours by the time 3rd platoon reached us. We all had a good laugh at them and never told them that we got the ride, just that we had arrived 8 hours prior.

On Christmas Eve we got word that we were

getting picked up the next day to return to BAF. Well Merry Freakin' Christmas. I couldn't ask for a better gift and I know that there wasn't a Ranger out there thinking any differently. The officers met with the town elders and informed them that we would be leaving. One of the elders pointed up into the mountains "Are those guys leaving too?" The people he was referring to was our LERPS (nickname for long range reconnaissance patrol) teams who had been up there for the last couple of weeks hoping to catch those who were trying to avoid us down below. We thought we had tricked them but they knew the entire time. Haji knows all!

As the Chinook landed, the loadmaster stepped off wearing to our surprise, a Santa costume. Are you kidding me?! We've been out here enduring this hell for the last month and this Air Force guy has the balls to show up dressed as Santa. Everyone was thinking the same thing but no one said anything. After the Old Saint Nick had briefed us and turned to walk back to the chopper, I barely caught a glimpse of it out of the corner of my eye before it reached him. Some Ranger had pegged him with a huge snowball. The loadmaster turned to glare at us but the entire group was border line rolling on the ground laughing. He chose wisely to ignore it and we had a safe trip to BAF.

Immediately when we got to BAF we were told to cut our hair before we showered. This didn't sit well. Hell, it was Christmas day and we all wanted hot chow. My Ranger buddies and I got our hair cut and cleaned up and headed to the chow hall to see what damage we could do. All of us were somewhat down for some reason I never understood. The food wasn't the best, but it was real and hot. As we sat down at the table I guess we all must have had a glum look on our faces because as the SGM passed by he said, "Hey Rangers, why do you look so down? Look at it this way, in 17 days you'll be home..." This was all news to us, and we began smiling. "...or you can look at it as we will be back in 47 days." Our faces dropped back. What did he just say? There's no way he said what I think he said. That means we will only be home for 30 days. I doubt we will even get leave. He had to be kidding, right?!

But the good news day wasn't over. We had learned that it was true that we were heading home in 17 days but returning to The Ghan in 47 days was speculation because that was our original rotation period. Remember we had only come because "we knew where Bin Ladin was." Our commander decided he didn't want us sitting around getting fat for 17 days I guess, so he volunteered us for one last mission. No one else had volunteered because no one else wanted it. The plan called for us to return to the same region that we had just left, by the cover of night, in Chinooks. Flying a Chinook in this terrain at night was very dangerous and only 160th SOAR would even be considered to fly the mission. That was a good feeling because I knew that 160th SOAR was the best damned rotor wing unit in the military. Anyway they would drop us off and we would start clearing towns for about 10 miles then return to the pick up point and come home. After the Chinooks dropped us at night, they would continue to circle above flooding the valley with IR which would only be visible to those with night vision. Sounded like a cool mission. Actually it sounded like a cold mission, but I had no idea how cold.

It was a dark, dark night even with my NOD's on I couldn't see anything inside of the Chinook. As we came upon the drop off site I heard the most frightening thing you can hear in that type of situation, "ROPES!!" What? The mission had not called for us to fast rope in, though we always know it is a possibility. This time we had to rope because it was way too dark to see the ground so the chopper could not land, only get us close. Everyone quickly got off their ruck and started putting their ropin' gloves on. I was all the way to the back of the packed to capacity Chinook. Everybody bumping into each other caused them to drop their gloves. It was chaos. When we got our

138

gloves on, we began trying to stand up which was a task it itself. Once standing then you had to get your ruck on. It was a mess. Finally it seemed we were all standing and had our rucks on. I couldn't see anything, but I could sense that all the shuffling around had stopped.

After standing using the advantage of being in the back to lean back against the wall I reached out to touch the guy in front of me to see where he was. Nothing. Oh shit, I guess we're moving, I shuffled a few feet forward grasping empty darkness. Oh shit, where is everybody? A bad feeling came over me; no way I missed the rope. I picked up the pace forward and then all of the sudden I could see the chem. stick that was taped to mark the rope. Oh shit, I thought right as the loadmaster saw me, "GOOOO!!!" I lunged at the glowing light hoping to find rope...there it is. The helicopter was already moving but barely. It was only about a 15 to 20 foot rope but with the Chinook moving it hurt. Just my luck, roped right into a creek. Freaking out too much to pay attention to the cold water that had just soaked me, I got up and was running in the direction of the scanning lasers. Only about 50 feet I reached my platoon sergeant. "Wiggins, there you are. Let's go." Is all he said.

It only took about half an hour of taking a knee waiting for the movement for me to reach that uncontrollable shaking state again. Shit I thought, every time, can you believe my luck! My team leader came over and took a knee beside my slapping me on the shoulder.

"You alright Wiggins...what in the hell, why are you soaked?"

Shuddering I managed to spout out, "I landed in a creek on the rope Sergeant."

"What in the hell Wiggins. You have the worst luck," my team leader chuckled. I wanted to punch him in the face ,but one, I couldn't see his face and two, I couldn't feel my hands. "You'll warm up when we start moving in a few minutes," he assured me. I wanted to start moving now, or lay down and die. I can't believe I signed up for this shit. At this point I couldn't wait for the re-enlistment NCO to contact me. Boy did I have something for him. Same old story that night, hurry up and wait. We didn't move for what seemed like hours. My eyes were getting heavy. There's no way I was falling asleep; I had slept all day in prep for the mission. I guessed I was dying. At that point; I didn't care, I was so tired of being cold all of the time.

We finally started moving and clearing which I thought would take my mind off being cold but it didn't. And finally the sun came up which I thought would warm me up, but it didn't. Late in the afternoon we set up a perimeter and set up to eat and get some rest. I changed my DCU's into my one clean set I had brought, even though it wasn't on the packing list. Thank God, for once something good. I never really warmed up that entire mission. Nothing big happened on that mission, but we did take out a few low ranking enemy soldiers. Actually they aren't soldiers, that is giving them more credit than they are worth. They are terrorists.

We returned to BAF unscathed but morale was at an all time low. Sometime just before we returned home it happened. U.S. forces announced that they had found Saddam Hussain inside a spider hole. This lifted everyone's spirits momentarily. We returned to the states only to find out a week later that the rumors were true. We would be going back to The Ghan in less than a month. We got one week leave and I spent it in Florida resting. Truthfully for once I didn't even feel like partying. I told myself I just have to make through the rest of this year and I am out. There was no way in hell I was re-enlisting, not for this shit.

I was not the only one so down; it seemed everyone was. After all, nothing truly significant had happened with the war on terror in a long time. Re-enlistment rates were at an all time low, and many Rangers were leaving regiment to join the conventional Army. The deployments had just become too much. Not only was it hard on the Rangers, but their families also. It seemed that by the time we were just getting settled in back home, it was time to go again. It's hard on families I imagine. Some Rangers had just got to the point where they wanted one 18 month deployment and then to know that they were done. The conventional Army could offer them that.

The night before Christmas
I'm stuck here in hell
No stocking stuffers
And no jingle bells
The jack-frost is nipping
But there's no Christmas tree
Lots of friends
But no family
Half a million soldiers
Fighting the terrorists
For those who aren't forgotten
For those sorely who're missed
The holidays are hard
For those soldiers stuck over here
So far away from loved ones
It's hard to find your cup of cheer
But we know why we're here
And we remember the reason
Because without our freedom
What good is a "season"
So tomorrow when you're celebrating
And the family is all together
Tell them not to worry
And read them all my letter
Happy holidays to all
I miss you for what it's worth
I'm on the other side of the world
Fighting for peace on Earth
Please don't worry about me
I promise I'm fine
And all of you are with me
In heart, soul, and mind
So have a very merry Christmas
And a happy new year
Be safe and I love you
You're the reason I'm here

O.E.F. 5

The prep for this deployment, for me at least, wasn't as bad as previous deployments. Regiment had decided to keep all of my chem. equipment in The Ghan last deployment and it saved me a huge headache. This did lift my spirits some because if I would have had to inventory everything that I had just recounted for the previous deployment, knowing it had not been touched, it would have pissed me off to no end. I wasn't even suppose to deploy with the Rangers this time.

Savannah had held a huge rugby tournament two weeks before deployment. The Rangers decided to field a team even though none of us knew anything about rugby. All we knew was we got to hit people. My platoon sergeant had told me not to play because he did not want to chance me getting hurt due to the fact that we were so short manned. I told this to the Battalion Commander, who was also playing, and he said to play, so I played. Everyone played balls to the wall and we even won a few games. Unfortunately the following Monday I saw half of the team at sick call. This included me and the B.C. The B.C. as it turned out, tore something in his knee and I had broken my wrist. When I returned to the company with a cast on my arm, my platoon sergeant went nuts.

"What in the hell happened Wiggins?" SSG Depouli demanded. I should have lied but I thought I was in the right.

"I broke my wrist playing rugby this weekend Sergeant," I reported.

"What the fuck Wiggins I told you not to

143

play?!" SSG Depouli was getting very angry.

Without thinking I said "The B.C. made me play sergeant." SSG Depouli shouted, "Fuck!!!" And turned around and stomped off. I knew that if someone asked the B.C. if he made me play I might be in for a world of shit, but for once I lucked out and no one did. So it was decided by the P.A. that I would remain on rear detachment (Rear D). I had heard horror stories about Rear D. CQ (commander of quarters) every other day, all kinds of shit details. I honestly didn't care because at least I would be warm at night and have hot food. I began to feel like I was really letting everyone down as I saw my guys getting ready to deploy. SSG Depouli approached me in a very calm manner.

"Wiggins they say it's up to you if you want to deploy, you can. We need you buddy." Shit, man, a guilt trip, come on man.

"I'll pack my shit today sergeant," I said in a not so enthused voice. So what I was told would happen is I would go to BAF with my guys and then they would go out on their mission and I would stay and pull TOC guard. Boring, but at least I would be warm at night and have hot food.

As I was making the rounds through my pre-deployment physical at every station the different medics would question the cast on my arm, and I would tell them I was ok, even though I wasn't. Then the unexpected occurred. I failed the audio logy portion of the exam. (This will seem ironic towards the end of the story.) The doctor told me technically that he shouldn't allow me to deploy. I look back and wonder if God was maybe trying to tell me to sit this deployment out. It took some convincing but I talked him into a re-test after the deployment. As much as I really didn't want to deploy I knew that once a hearing problem was documented I would probably be Released For Medical. I loved the Rangers I had absolutely no urge to be in the conventional army.

Not a week after we arrived in Afghanistan:
"Wiggins we are going out to Tarmac farms (the range in Afghanistan) to sight in the .50 cals, can you help out?" SSG Depouli asked. SSG Depouli wasn't usually nice about anything and he never asked, he always told, so I said sure. When we returned from the range SSG Depouli asked me, "How did that feel?" What the hell is going on since when in the hell has SSG Depouli ever cared about how I felt?

"A lil rough," I responded as I rubbed my wrist.

"You know Wiggins we are really short manned and don't have any other top gunners. Do you think you could handle a drive down to Skhin?" SSG Depouli asked. Wait that almost sounded like a compliment. Most guys joked that SSG Depouli was bi-polar because he would randomly go nuts on someone for seemingly no reason. Not knowing what to say "I could probably handle that sergeant." Dammit I had been conned into doing what I said I wouldn't, but SSG Depouli was being nice to me.

We had about a week to prep our gear and fuck off with no training whatsoever. One day I was shuffling back to my tent from chow when I spotted "the stance." There was only one person I have ever met who stood like that. He was a statue of authority. Just seeing him stand there like that could make a weak man tremble. "Sergeant Holmes?" I shouted. He turned to me. Holy shit, I was right. He wore a full thick beard that told me one thing...he had moved on to bigger and better things. "Sergeant Holmes! How goes it? So what, are you in Delta now?" I asked. He just replied "nope" and walked off. BADASS!

The day we mounted up to head out I slapped a patch onto my uniform that read: "Terrorists hunt them, find them, kill them." It had a picture of Bin Laden in iron sights and everyone thought it was the shit. Everyone that is except for SFC Lonnie. He yelled at me and made me remove it. What a dickhead I thought, and I was already regretting signing up for the mission.

I began regretting it much more about the third

146

day of driving across rough desert terrain. SSG Depouli had told me it was all paved roads to Shkin. I should have known better. Once again I found myself freezing on the top gun with nowhere to go and on top of that, every pothole and berm was putting a new crack in my wrist. When we reached Shkin I thought to myself "finally done," but this compound was definitely no BAF as I had been told it was. I found out quickly that the mechanics had plans for me during my stay at Shkin, Preventive Maintenance Checks and Services, the worst detail in the Army if you ask me. As my guys prepared to head out on their mission I was hearing that the plan was to rotate three days out and one day back in compound to clean up and get some grub. I thought to myself, now that's not bad and I wouldn't have to do PMCS every day. Captain Sellers had been all but begging me to top gun for his jeep because there was just no one else to do it, but I had been telling him how the ride out here had hurt bad. "Hey CPT. Sellers my arm is much better. You got a top gunner if you still need one," I said grinning. I was in.

My Ranger group had split in two. One set up a vehicle check point to the north, and one to the south. Three days out one day in, yeah right. Everyone else got that deal but not the commander's vehicle. We stayed out pretty much the entire three months. We would rotate between blocking postions (BP's) instead of going back to Shkin. My commander is such a bad ass, I was going to kill him. After about a month of staring at the same mountain, one day I was walking around looking at the ground. Cpt. Sellers saw this and questioned me "Wiggins what are you doing?"

147

"Looking for a long stick sir," I replied.

"Wiggins you're in the dessert you probably aren't going to find a long stick. What in the hell do you need a long stick for anyways?" the Captain asked.

"I'm going to kill you with it sir. I'm going to take out the whole group and then when I'm done I'm going to turn the gun on myself, but I can't reach the butterfly (trigger on the .50 cal) so I need a long stick you see," I informed him not even cracking a smile. Captain Sellers just looked at me blankly and said, "Wiggins you're sick." I just sat around all day when I wasn't pulling guard eating MRE's getting fat as hell. No one messed with me because everyone knew I wasn't even supposed to be there. I didn't really give a fuck when I got back from this deployment I was just going to coast out my last six months.

"Hey Wiggins, you wanna walk up to the OP (observation point) with me," the commander asked. I figured what the hell. It was just a few hundred feet up. At least it would be a change of pace, and I hadn't been up there yet so I might as well check it out. Well that was a steep ass few hundred feet and Cpt. Sellers got there about ten minutes before me. "Goddamn Wiggins, you are getting out of shape. Walking doesn't hurt your hand. Every day you need to walk these guys fresh water up here," CPT Sellers ordered. Shit! I knew better. What's the first thing that you learn in the Army? Never volunteer for anything!

The view from the OP was very interesting. I had never been to Pakistan but I just assumed it was the same as Afghanistan; not so. From the OP looking down one side of the mountain I could see several local villages. Typical mud huts with no roof, dirty, no green trees, women washing "clothes" twenty feet down stream from where their kids are pissing in it, basic third world scenery. When I looked down the other side of the mountain into Pakistan it almost reminded me of home. I could see grass and trees, there was a paved road the house even looked almost normal from the distance. I thought wow how could there be this much of a difference on separate sides of one mountain.

We took a lot of indirect fire at that compound but never anything too serious. Every night we would send out a mounted patrol to drive up and down the Pakistan border to search for terrorists moving back and forth across the border. We didn't have a whole lot of success, and one day someone decided it was because they knew our routine. So on this night the plan was to send out the normal convoy except halfway out, everyone except the driver and top gunner would jump out and take cover and concealment. The jeeps would return to base making the enemy think that our mission for the night was over. I didn't care. It was a stupid idea. It would never work. Oh guess what? We don't have enough people. Wiggins we need you to be a top gunner. "Good." Yeah that was sarcasm. So off we went and I have to admit it went pretty smoothly considering the planning that went into it. When they got the word GO, everyone was off the vehicles and had disappeared within a matter of seconds. When the convoy turned around to RTB and we drove right back by where we had dropped off our guys, I couldn't even see them with my NOD's on....eerie. The convoy had just RTB when all hell broke loose. We were parking

149

the GMV's when someone ran out of the compound, "the guys are taking serious contact. You gotta go get them."

"Are you shitting me?!" Excitement, hadn't seen this in a while. We mounted up and hauled ass, I mean HAULED ASS, back to the guys. I didn't even notice how much the bumps were hurting my arm, my adrenalin was pumping so hard. As we came closer I could hear a lot of machine gun fire and explosions. Oh man this is the shit I live for, I thought to myself. We were turning the last corner as I realized that the firing had stopped. It was over. Just that quick the Rangers had annihilated the entire enemy force, and I missed it. It was just like the cadence goes, "Bodies Bloody Bodies." They were plenty and everywhere. How many Rangers were wounded you ask? ZERO. I had found something to be excited about again. There was still action to be seen in The Ghan. Here I was thinking that it was over.

The next week was very calm and I started to get down again. Every few days the guys would switch out, and we would remain. One night SPC Landers who was a Commo guy or radio boy, snickered on the way out, "Hey Wiggins, I'll be thinking about ya at chow tonight." That son of a bitch! The convoy didn't get 100 meters away before I heard them call in a medivac. What in the hell I thought. As it turned out, Landers who was sitting inside the jeep, was resting his hand inside the gun turret and for some reason the turret came loose and spun around and took Landers finger with it. I was told Landers screamed, "stop the jeep" and before it had stopped he had jumped out and was looking for his finger. I cringed, ouch. Then suddenly I found poetic justice in it all.

Yes! We are moving the BP's (blocking positions). Buh bye ugly mountain. I wont miss you. For some reason looking at that mountain had been driving me crazy. The new BP we were setting up was very well concealed with lots of trees. It gave nice shade from the sun during the day, and I liked it though it got a little cold at night which sucked during guard shift.

One night Ranger McColmes and I were sitting on guard whispering back and forth when something caught our eye. "Did you see that?" I asked.

"Hell yeah it was fast" McColmes replied. We got in the prone and began scanning with our lasers. All of the sudden from behind a tree a huge cat pounced onto the laser beam. "Holy Shit," I practically yelled. It's amazing that neither one of us fired.

"Is that a mountain lion?" McColmes asked me.

"It damn sure looked like it I didn't know there

were mountain lions in Afghanistan," I argued. "Well should we shoot it?" we both asked each other at the same time.

"I say no unless it attacks" was my argument. We lied there lasers on the big cat for what must have been five minutes. It seemed as though it could see the laser beams which was crazy because you are only supposed to be able to see those with night vision. He finally wandered off into the night, but what an experience.

Again at this BP we took indirect fire a couple of times, but not much went on. For some reason there were lots of animals though. We would just spend the day bullshitting when not pulling guard. Some Rangers such as SSG Depouli would do PT for hours. He finally started giving me shit about not doing any PT one day, and I told him I just wanted my wrist to completely heal first. He just glared at me. The worst was when SFC Lonnie came out to that BP. All he ever did was complain about something. One day he was going through his normal bitch fit and he started ranting "You know who don't belong in Regiment, SGM Devens. That motherfucker has no idea what the Ranger standard is." Wow, I thought. That is a bold statement. SMG Devens or SGM Grenada as we affectionately called him, was quite possibly the strongest hoss in Regiment and he had been around for longer than pretty much anyone else too. Not only that, but SMG Grenada was a great guy. He would sit around and bullshit with the lowest ranking private. He was nice, but man if you pissed him off you had better watch out. It made me smile to think of what SMG Grenada was going to do to Lonnie when I told him the shit he was talking. I would too; we had played rugby together and became pretty good friends. He was also a high school discus thrower, as was I, so we always talked shit back and forth. He'd try to tell me, "Wiggins, I could throw you farther than you can throw the discus." To which I'd reply, "That may be true but you will never throw the discus farther than me." He was strong but you need a lot more than strength to throw the discus. I know because I had whipped the shit out of 100 guys just like SGM Grenda before.

One day one of our convoys got split into and it couldn't have happened at a worse time. It was right in the middle of an ambush. We heard that a Ranger had been KIA and then the next day we found out who. Ranger Pat Tillman. Oh my God, no. Not only was Pat a really good guy and everybody loved him, but he was the last Ranger who could ever be KIA. Why? Because there was no way to keep it out of the media. We all knew right away it would be a big deal. Pat had turned down a multi million dollar pro football contract to join the Rangers with his brother and had become a modern day national hero. At the time I thought this is just what this country needs, a real hero, something to forget about Spiderman, which was a huge movie at the time. But when I had talked to Pat just a few days before I found myself asking him, "How could you turn down millions of dollars for this?" Pat just smiled.

A bunch of my guys took a road trip to Ft. Benning when Pat got to RIP just to smoke him. When they returned I asked them, "Did you smoke his arrogant ass?" Everyone concurred that no, they had not, and he was a really cool guy. At the time I thought they were just sell outs, but I learned that they were right.

During the fire fight Pat was caught in the cut off section of the convoy on the other side of the hill. Anxious to "go get some" he sprung from the GMV and rushed the hill and was fighting from the top. I guess some Ranger was not expecting another Ranger on that hill which is understandable, but still we are all taught to identify the target before we shoot. Pat had been killed by friendly fire. It was a sad day in our Nation, for the family, and for his brother Rangers.

We had rotated to the other BP to the south where the guys out there had commandeered an old abandoned farm house. We were running daily missions out of there and I was mostly pulling guard. Like always we would take sporadic gun fire from the surrounding mountains. One day my guard shift had just ended and I was walking away from the top gun where I had been replaced, when I heard distant gun fire. "Son of a bitch!!" my replacement yelled. I spun around as he grabbed his ear. They had winged his ear and he was pissed. He started firing the MK-19 across the Pakistani border. He finally stopped firing, but he didn't stop cursing for hours.

The next day some of our guys were on a mounted patrol flying down the Pakistan border blaring Skynard when they came screaming up on the Pakistan border patrol. Both parties caught by complete surprise were locked and loaded on each other. The Pakistanis had the advantage as they had bunkers with big ass machine guns, but they were out numbered. There was no way to tell that they were the border patrol as no one was in uniform. Finally one of the Pakistanis stepped forward and identified himself as the commander. He then demanded to know what we were doing. He insisted on speaking to our commander but, he was at the compound with me. He wanted to know why we had been firing on them and why we were crossing the border because we were not allowed to. He seemed very pissed off. The confrontation ended with a promise from our ranking guy to the Pakistani commander that they would return tomorrow with the commander. Everyone was irked by the commander's demands and how pissed off he seemed to be.

In the long run, CPT Sellers decided he would meet with the Pakistani commander. Everyone was expecting a shoot out including the Captain. The top gunners were told to point their weapons just off of the bunkers but to remain alert at all times. Two drivers, two top gunners, and one radio guy would remain at the compound. If all hell broke loose, we were to call in air support and the drivers and gunners were to head up for unexpected back up. Remember that old Army saying "Expect the worst, hope for the best," well that was in full effect on this mission. The five of us sat at the compound anxiously waiting and fully expecting any moment of silence to burst into hell. As the convoy pulled up to the same spot as yesterday where the border patrol had been, they immediately noticed that there were a lot more people and they were all in uniform. Not good. The environment was very intense and the bunker guns were locked onto the GMV's the entire time the two commanders talked. CPT Sellers assured the Pakistani commander that we had not crossed the border. The Pakistani commander then told CPT Sellers "You are across the border right now." I don't know how the rest of the conversation went that day, but it all ended safely without a shot being fired. I will never forget it.

The days and weeks droned on and all of the action seemed to be taking place in this little wood bazaar just south of us. Every time we sent someone down there it would end in a fire fight. By this time my arm was feeling much better and I was much more active in the missions. One day I got chosen for the OP team. An OP or Observation Point is usually set up a few hundred meters on either side of a compound to pull guard and make sure that no one is sneaking up on you. OP Club One, they named it after a gay club back in Savannah, was located on a hilltop about 500 meters north and 500 feet up from the compound. I liked it up there because I was with people that I liked and it was peaceful with a beautiful view. On the third night up there I had already taken one guard shift and was sleeping peacefully when Mcglaghlin awoke me whispering, "Wiggins get up we got movement." How gay I thought to myself. It's probably just a farmer on an early start into town. I figured if I had to wake up I'd do my good buddy Kvam the favor of waking him up too. We put on our gear and climbed out of the bunker while SGT Fitz was telling us he could see a couple of them, and they had fire arms. Yeah…yeah I thought to myself. Just as I flipped down my NOD's, I saw the flash of the first shot ring out of SGT Fitz' M4.

It all happened at once as I scanned for what he was shooting at, I realized there were people shooting at us. Kvam and I began moving and shooting. It was hard because there were trees everywhere. Kvam and I moved out so that the trees were not in our way and that's when we realized all hell was breaking lose and they were everywhere! I could hear bullets whizzing by my head and yet so much was happening I didn't even realize we were standing right out in the open. We weren't even five minutes into the firefight and both Kvam and I were on our second mag already. I was trying to pick targets with my NOD's not paying any attention to Kvam, when suddenly I realized I was alone. Shit, where was Kvam?! I fired a few more shots. Then I heard Kvam screaming my name. Oh no I thought, I hope he's ok. I looked in the direction of the screaming and realized everyone was in the bunker and they were trying to get me in there too. I ran and dove into the bunker. Mclaughlin who was a forward observer was on the radio trying to get mortars. There was so much radio traffic he couldn't even get through. SGT Fitz told Kvam and me to provide him cover fire so that he could fire the Gustov at the next hilltop where a bunch on fire was coming from.

I was halfway through my third mag when my M4 jammed. I tried and tried and tried but had no luck getting the round un-jammed. "Kvam, lemme see your leatherman," I screamed in desperation. We could hear the enemy making its way up the side of the hill and all I could think was we were going to be over run and I was going to be sitting here trying to un-jam my weapon. Finally that son of a bitch round flipped out. I slapped the mag back in and looked up just in time to see a sizzling on the ground. "Frag!!" I yelled. We all hit the deck in the bunker. No explosion, at least not three feet in front of us. I peeked over the edge...nothing. Back to work.

Mclaughlin kept trying to raise someone on the radio, SGT Fitz was putting Gustov rounds on the hilltop, and Kvam and I were taking care of all of the rest.

"Kvam, buddy, this may seem crazy, but this is the shit I live for!" I screamed over an explosion.

"Hell yeah man," was what I got in return.

"Mclaughlin, you havin' any luck with the radio," SGT Fitz was getting worried.

"Negative Sergeant. Everyone is trying to talk at the same time," Mac informed him. SGT Fitz dropped the Gustov and hopped into the bunker, grabbed the mike from Mac and screamed, "Everyone shut the fuck up so we can get some goddamn mortars on the bad guys!" There was a second of silence on the radio and then, "Ok what you got Mac?" the mortars asked. Mac spouted off some grid numbers followed by "Drop 50 fire for effect!"

"Fuck yeah that's what I like to hear Mac!" I yelled back at him. Kvam, Fitz, and I continued fighting but the Gustov was done, all rounds spent. Speaking of which, I was running out of ammo fast.

"Kvam, buddy, how much ammo you got left?" I asked hoping he had plenty to spare.

"Two mags, you?" Not the answer I was hoping for.

"One full mag in the weapon and one mag in kit."

"Guys they say they can't put mortars on the coordinates. They are saying it is right on top of us," Mac informed us.

"Well damn tell them that's where the bad guys are!" I was getting pissed off. We were about to be over ran.

"Fuck it, I'm gonna toss some grenades down the side of the mountain," was the best I could come up with. I climbed out of the bunker trying to manage my weapon. I wanted to leave it in the bunker so that I could get better distance, but I had a bad feeling I might need it and hell, I didn't need to get that much distance anyway. So no shit, there I was running, shooting, and trying to prep a grenade all at the same time. "Frag out," I yelled. And threw it as far as I could. It felt like it landed 10 feet in front of me. I was all wrapped up in my weapon and didn't get any distance with it. I

159

waited for the explosion...nothing. What in the hell? I pulled out another grenade and got some good distance this time...boom! I said "oh yeah that got a hold of some haji." It was my last grenade and I climbed back into the bunker high fiving Kvam on the way in. Kvam said "I'm gonna throw mine."

"The more the merrier." I assured him. Kvam threw his two grenades down the side of the mountain and we laughed at what it must have been doing. I was half way through my last mag as the sun was coming up and Mac handed me two of his. He had spent most of the time on the radio. I had also threw his two grenades. What can I say it was fun.

By sun up the fire fight had died down and air support was en route. The four of us took off our NOD's and decided to go on the offensive. We weren't sure where the enemy had disappeared to, so we were low crawling, which sucked. Then another bad feeling overcame us. We could hear the jets approaching. There were trees everywhere and there was no way to make out that we were coalition forces. The Air Force knew where the Ranger compound was but not about our OP. We decided to attach bright orange markers to our backs in hopes that they would be able to tell we were the good guys. Air support obviously had their eyes on something because they were tearing up the next two hills over. They would swing through and fire thousands of rounds in a matter of just a few seconds and drop a bomb or two, then circle around to do it again. After about an hour of that the planes RTB. Now it was time to sweep.

The platoons from the compound began patrols

to search stragglers or wounded enemy while we followed their movement from the OP. The sun had been up for a couple of hours, and now we could see the damage that had been caused. Our entire bunker was destroyed by small arms fire but miraculously none of us had been hit. That sizzling I had seen right in front of the bunker that night was a round for the Gustov. It had been hit by enemy fire. If it would have gone off right at that spot, it would have killed all of us. Somehow we lucked out the round went through the back where I guess the gun power was located and instead of detonating is just burned off. There were literally hundreds of holes in the trees all around us.

The guys were still sweeping the area and were finding some bodies but not nearly as many as expected. However that day we found dozens of unfired RPG's that they never got a chance to shoot, and some AK's. There were blood trails everywhere that showed the damage that we had done to them, but it seemed as though they must have carried off at least some of their wounded or dead. The teams were moving through the brush now, and we couldn't really follow their movement anymore, so we were inspecting our gear and OP. Suddenly five or six shots rang out. "I guess they found someone." I smiled. Looking at the back of the bunker there were holes all in it too. "What in the hell, they were behind us too?" Kvam was puzzled. So was I.

OP Club One from left to right:
SPC Kvam, PFC McLaughlin, SGT Fitz

Looking down from OP Club One
onto the RGR compound

Another hour or two passed and then I spotted the commander and Chaplin coming up the trail.

"Wiggins, what in the hell did you do up here?" CPT Sellers rang out. I dropped to my knees and threw my hands into the air, mocking the movie *Boondock Saints*. "It was a fire fight!!!" I screamed at the top of my lungs. Every Ranger loves the movie *Boondock Saints,* so everyone knew what I was talking about and we all had a good laugh. Then we told the commander the story as it had happened from beginning to end.

"Damn sir I guess they were behind us too, because there are bullet holes all in the back of the bunker," I told him.

"Well you're right, in a sense, there were bad guys on the back side of the compound firing into the compound but I suspect that the rounds in the bunker came from us," CPT Sellers said.

"What?!" all four of us seem to stammer at the same time.

"We figured because the shots were coming from this hilltop so heavily that you guys must have been overrun. Then when we couldn't get radio contact with you for over an hour, we were all sure that you were dead." Sellers told the story.

"Well thanks for the confidence sir!" we were all saying.

We went on to show him the area and how close we had come to actually being overrun. Some of the blood trails were not 50 feet from the bunker. I told the CO if he were smart, he would get the re-enlistment officer up there right now. I would have seriously signed the contract on the spot. This was what I lived for. I would never find this kind of adventure as a civilian. What the hell was I thinking when I said I would never re-up?

163

In the after action review (AAR) it was speculated by everyone that there were approximately 50 enemy combatants there that night. Their plan was to set up and attack at dawn. It could have been a massacre. They were setting up on the high ground and the compound was several hundred feet below, very vulnerable. The damage was bad enough as it was. Several of the vehicles were down, every vehicle had holes in them, and several Rangers had to be medivaced for small injuries.

OP Club One had saved the day and we were all awarded valorous medals. Mine reads: "For exceptional heroism while serving as a nuclear biological chemical specialist in support of Operation Enduring Freedom. On this date, Specialist Wiggins' actions and courage under enemy fire contributed to the overall success of the Joint Task Force. His dedication to duty, commitment to excellence, and selfless acts of bravery without regard for his own safety were instrumental in fighting off an enemy attack, which saved his personnel and its mission. Through his distinctive accomplishments, Specialist Wiggins reflected great credit upon himself, this command, and the United States Army." Awarded by Major General Stanley A. McChrystal.

General McChrystal and I had met several times and this would not be the last. One time that I will never forget, he had came up to Khoust to make an assessment and was walking around. You never salute in a combat zone, but when he walked by me I snapped to attention. He then turned to me and asked, "Hey Ranger, have you seen any terrorist around here?" I tried so hard to keep from smiling but was unsuccessful. "No sir not really." He replied, "Damn, I don't understand, I really thought there would be some up here."

We had received orders to move north into the vicinity that Ranger Tillman had been killed in a few weeks prior. We spent the day breaking down the BP which was a pain in the ass because after what had now become known as the infamous firefight at BP209, we had filled thousands of sand bags and bunkers around the compound. We certainly weren't going to leave them for the enemy to use, so we had to empty all of them. It was a long day and I was glad to finally be mounting up to leave. We were finally moving and I looked over BP209 one last time. Wow, it sure looked different than it did when we first arrived. Best I remember it was a fairly clear night, bumpy as always, but I had grown used to that a long time ago. I was scanning ridgelines to the left with my .50 cal and laser when it happened. **BOOM!!!** I couldn't move or speak. I heard SSG Depouli screaming my name, probably wondering why I wasn't shooting. I remember thinking, so this is what it's like to die. Then just as quickly as I was brought into the world, I was gone.

Obviously I don't remember the rest of this day, so I have called on one of my Ranger buddies to give their account of exactly what happened. Who better than my good Ranger buddy, Ranger Tony Kvam. I did not change one word of what he wrote because lets face it anybody is a better writer than I am. So without further ado, Ranger Toney Kvam:

I remember the day my Ranger buddy, Tom Wiggins, was wounded. Not only was he my Ranger buddy but he was also my roommate at the time. To this day he is still one of my best friends. The day was just like any other day, boring, yet peaceful. A week earlier them Haji fuckers tried to be sneaky and attack us while we were sleeping. They didn't know that Wiggins, Fitz, Mac, and I were up on an OP pulling guard. The same OP they decided to walk up on and plan their attack, dumb asses! It was probably around 70 to 80 degrees, not a cloud in the sky. The scenery was incredible. We were surrounded by endless hilltops, mountains, trees you name it. Afghanistan I will admit is a beautiful country if you're not walking or driving through one of its shit-hole towns. Or getting shot at! We were located along the border of Pakistan. You could see the Pakistani border patrol through the ACOG of your M4. Ranger Wiggins and I, along with 3rd platoon and a few detachments from mortars and recon platoons, were operating out of an abandoned farm house that was dug into the side of a hill. The two houses were more like caves. I was an assistant gunner in the anti tank squad and Wiggins was assigned as a top gunner on a .50 cal. SGT Fitz was our team leader and SSG Depouli was our platoon sergeant. We like to call him Delta Depouli for his hard nose attitude toward everything. Every fucking fire fight that 1st Ranger Battalion had been in since the war started in 2001 he had been in it. He knew his shit and Wiggins and I looked up to him even when he was in our face smoking the shit out of us or just telling us we were fuck ups. This was my last deployment; my ETS (estimated time of separation) date was only two months away.

The day started out the same as every day.

Everyone just gets into a routine to the point where it just becomes natural. We'd wake up, eat an MRE, do hygiene, and then sit around and bullshit for the rest of the day. Well, not all day, because the bullshit sessions would get interrupted by having to pull guard shifts or go on a patrol through the mountains. If it wasn't for patrols or guard shifts we'd sit on MRE boxes and lay on the sand bagged mortar pits all day long and tell stories about nights on the town in Savannah, Ga. Not everyone just sat around all the time. We'd do PT at least once a day to keep in shape. Then once in a while our platoon sergeants would make us practice CQB (close quarters battles) or give classes to the privates.

On this day we had received orders to move further north and relieve 2nd Batt. so they could go back to the states. The area we were headed was the same area Pat Tillman had been killed a few weeks earlier in an ambush. We started taking down all of our fortified positions by dumping and destroying the sand bags we had build up after the intense fire fight a few weeks earlier. We finished up and sat around waiting again to move out. "Hurry up and wait" was the theme every day. SFC Dillingham, the mortar platoon sergeant had his laptop hooked up to some speakers, so we sat around listening to music from the 80's. He was a big fan of 80's music. I remember the last song we listened to before we rolled out that day was West End Girls by The Pet Shop Boys. The sun was just below the mountains as we started to load up the GMV's. I made sure that the new privates who had just arrived a couple days prior, Fletcher and Gerleski, had their shit squared away before we left. They didn't need much direction, they were sharp, and caught on quick. I had all the confidence in them. Fletcher was a 34 year old cowboy from Alpine, Texas and Gerleski was a young 19 year old out of Ohio. It was my job to make sure that they knew the ropes. We got everything loaded up and all the vehicles were in line waiting to move out. I was riding in a Toyota Hylux with SGT FItz and SFC Dillingham was the driver. Wiggins was riding top gun as usual and had SSG Depouli, Fletcher, Gerleski, SGT Jaeger, TSGT Hurst, and Cpt. Sellers. Depouli was driving, Sellers was the TC, Jaeger and Hurst were sitting behind them and the new privates were in the back with the equipment.

The sky was clear and you could see the stars shining overhead. The ride was a bit bumpy as usual but pretty quiet. Ten minutes went by and we started slowing down a bit. Suddenly there was a loud explosion followed by the cracking of automatic gun fire. Tracers rounds lit up the sky as they wizzed overhead. "Why the fuck are we stopped? We usually drive through this shit," SFC Dillingham was asking himself. I stuck my M4 out the window and began firing at the wood piles to my left. I wanted to lay down cover fire in case the enemy was behind the wood piles. We had no idea where the shots were coming from. I continued to lay down suppressive fire so that we could all get out of the vehicle. It was obvious now that we weren't going anywhere soon. SFC Dillingham got out and linked up with his mortar guys. SGT Fitz and I got out and took cover behind the wood pile. "Where the fuck are these shots coming from, do you see anybody?" Fitz asked. "Negative sergeant" I replied. Fitz then told me to get the round for the Gustav out from the back of the truck. He continued to lay down suppressive fire while I stood up to grab the rounds for the Gustav. I grabbed the rounds and returned to Fitz immediately. I was instructed to load a round.

"Back blast area clear, Gustav going hot!" I yelled so that everyone around us could hear that we were about to unleash the fury. I could hear someone screaming in pain about 100 meters to my left. Fitz and I knew that one of our guys had been fucked up.

We shot off a few more rounds from the Gustav and then continued to stay behind cover. Things were starting to quiet down at this point. It was no longer necessary to be firing our weapons. By this time we had line squads from 3rd platoon sweeping through the high ground that surrounded us. We could still hear the screams from a wounded Ranger buddy nearby, but we knew that he was being taken care of by the medics so we continued to pull security. I remember thinking those fuckers picked the perfect spot to nail us. The road started to wind like a snake and there were wood piles everywhere and we had to zigzag around the wood piles. There was a little concrete house of the left side of the road and the high ground all around us was thick with trees. Here we were on the low ground in between two hills. It was the perfect place to attack. The enemy could hit us without ever being seen, not to mention they would have all sorts of cover and concealment. It was obvious now that we had been ambushed and one of our guys was hit, but we didn't know anything else.

While sitting there pulling security I heard SSG Depouli's voice "Kvam buddy, where ya at?" "Here sergeant." I replied. He came over to where Fitz and I were pulling security and told Fitz to go link up with Fletch and Geleski. He had me go with him and he led me to SGT Hurst who was an Air Force ETAC and was always attached to us. He had become one of us in no time. He was sitting up against a wood pile with a bandage over *his eye. He had cuts all over his face but he was as calm as could be. Depouli told me to talk to him, so I did. I asked him if he needed anything responded with, "No I'm fine" in the most casual voice. I thought to myself what a tough son of a bitch that guy was.*

I could now see that the guy screaming was SGT Jaeger. The medics were working on him while we screamed out "THOSE MOTHERFUCKERS I'M GONNA KILL THEM!" He had taken shrapnel from an airburst RPG all up and down both arms and legs. Eventually Depouli came back and told me to walk Hurst over to his vehicle. It was clear now that Wiggins' vehicle had pretty much been destroyed by RPG's. Once I got TSGT Hurst sitting down Depouli had me come with him. He brought me where Wiggins was lying silently as the medics worked on him. "Hey this is his best friend right here let him get in there." Depouli commanded. The medics had me take Wiggins hand and told me to keep him staying with us by having him squeeze my hand. So that's what I did. "Squeeze my hand Tom," I'd say over and over again. "Hang in there we are gonna get you out of here." Chaplin Bowlus was to my left saying prayers while Doc Pairimore and Delk the medic from HHC worked on Wiggins. "Come on man, we still got a lot of parties to attend to in Gainesville man." I pleaded with Wiggins.

Wiggins was from Hawthorne, Florida a small town outside of Gainesville. Wiggins and I would take road trips on occasion to hang out and party. Wiggins hooked me up with a girl there that I lost my virginity too. Wiggins was the man when it came to women. He is one of the funniest people I know. Women like guys who can make them laugh. I thought about how weird it was going to

*be to lose him after living with him for the last 4
months and hanging out all the time. Then I
thought about how we would joke about one of us
getting hit while being deployed. How ironic that it
happened and that it wasn't a joke anymore.*

*I kept repeating "come on Tom, squeeze my
hand bud, squeeze my hand. You're a tough
bastard you're not going anywhere do you hear
me." Sometimes he would give me a squeeze
sometimes he wouldn't. Suddenly he lost his pulse
and then I heard the Chaplin begin the prayer:
"As I walk through the valley of the shadow and
death I shall fear no evil." The Chaplin preached
on. I knew this was not a good sign. Was this the
last time I would see my friend, lying on his back
in some shit hole combat zone torn up from an
RPG? I sure hoped fucking not! I did not want to
see him die in Afghanistan. Thank God he
regained his pulse. "You fucker quit playin' with
us," Doc Pairemore said. As it turned, out
Wiggins had been slipping back and forth to the
other side. "That a boy!" I said "You're not
going anywhere; we got a lot of stuff to do when
we get back man."*

*Finally an hour and a half after Wiggins was
hit, the medivac arrived. Pairimore said, "Let's
get him up." Chaplin Bowlus, SSG Depouli, and I
lifted the stretcher and carried Wiggins to the
Blackhawk that was waiting to take him away
along with Hurst, Jaeger, and Sellers. Cpt. Sellers
had taken some shrapnel to the face and hands.
We got Wiggins and everyone else loaded in the
Blackhawk. I ended up being stuck in the chopper,
so in order to get out I had to climb over Jaeger.
So I quickly placed my hand on him and stepped
over him. He screamed out in pain. I felt bad but I
had no other way to get out otherwise. I was quick
about it though, so I don't think it was too bad for*

him, at least I hoped it wasn't. I was out and the medivac took off. Depouli then told me I would be top gunning for Wiggins the rest of the deployment.

I sat there on that .50 cal that night staring into a fire that broke out in a wood pile from an RPG round. The flames were huge. They had to be roaring twenty feet into the air at least I thought. Something exploded in the fire and for a second I thought "here we go again." There were a couple more explosions through the night and it kept me alert, that's for sure. I put in a Copenhagen and sat there pulling guard on that .50 cal and watching the IR strobes flash from third platoon who was still sweeping the hill. I sat there till sun up. It was just way too quiet after all of the shit that had just happened. I saw Fletcher, "How you doing?" I asked.

"Good, I got grazed by shrapnel, check this out," he said pulling down his collar enough so that I could see the wound on his shoulder."

"Nice" I said. Fletcher had been the one who pulled TSGT Hurst behind cover after he had fallen off the vehicle. He is going to be a good Ranger, I could tell. Everyone on Wiggins' vehicle got hit except Depouli and Gereleski. Now that the sun was up I could see blood stains all over the roof of the vehicle I was on. I knew it was Wiggins's. I hope he's going to be alright I thought. I hope they are all going to be ok.

The strangest thing about the ambush was that during the sweep they found nothing. No casings, no RPG launchers, no clothing, nothing. It was as if we were attacked by ghosts. They vanished without a trace. Did we just imagine this shit? Were we all out of our flippin' minds? How could they just disappear without leaving anything behind. That was the weirdest part of it all. After the incident on the OP a few weeks ago, we found shit left behind everywhere. Honestly who has time to pick up brass during a fire fight?

The next day we got news on our boys. Sellers would be returning to us and the rest of the guys were being flown to Germany. We were told TSGT Hurst had lost an eye, SGT Jaeger would have to have extensive surgery to repair damaged skin and muscle tissue, and as for Wiggins, no one was sure. I continued on through the rest of the deployment and made it home safely. It sure was different without having Wiggins or the rest of the guys around anymore. When I got back to the States the room was as quiet as it had ever been. It was weird not having Wiggins there. Normally we would walk through the door together, not this time.

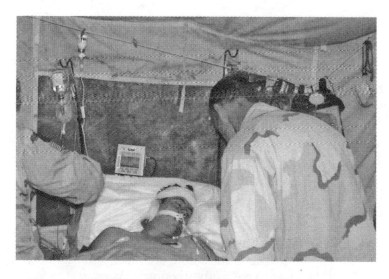

General McCrystal pinning a purple heart on Wiggins in a make shift hospital

He swore the last time was the last time
He'd be walkin' down that flightline
But being married to a Ranger
Is like being married to a stranger
All she knows is what he told her
While she was cryin' on his shoulder
I love, I'll miss you and I'll be home soon
Expect a letter every afternoon
Then he got on another Airplane
Headed somewhere else insane
Off to ease other people's pain
With nothing more for him to gain
While he's gone his world stops spinning
But back home new life's beginning
It's hard to write him everyday
With the baby on the way
'Cause there's so much to do
And baby I miss you
And I can't wait until I see the day
When there'll be no more airplanes
'Cause they're drivin' me insane
Please come home and ease my pain
We have the world to gain
Everyday she meets the mailman
And he puts his letter in her hand
But today another uniformed man
Says I'm truly sorry ma'am
And she starts to go insane
Screamin' goddamn those airplanes
All they do is cause so much pain
But who the hell should she blame
'Cause she's proud of all he did
And she's proud of how he lived
And she can't wait until she sees the day
Her son gets on his first airplane
Headed somewhere else insane
Off to ease other people's pain
You know we have the world to gain

Not a Good Day to Die

I spent the next two months slipping in and out of consciousness. I may have been opening my eyes but I certainly was not seeing reality. At the time I thought I was though. The first time that I remembered anything I thought that I was in India. An Indian doctor was looking over me. He then proceeded to pull out a buck knife and cut skin from his back. When he had gotten what he wanted he then grafted it onto me. I was supposedly conscious during this entire operation. When he was done I thanked him.

Then I began thinking that the nurses were conspiring to kill me. At this point a believed I was in England. One day I came to for a second while one of the nurses was doing something to me and started screaming that she was trying to kill me, but there was nothing I could do as I was strapped down. I saw my family standing there, watching this nurse, making sure that she wasn't killing me? When I was alone in the room and I would grow conscious, I could feel some one pulling my calves down pinning me to the bed and I could see a huge knife coming out from under the bed to kill me. I would scream for help and they would let my calves go. This went on for what seemed like forever. I mean wow, to think there is always someone right there trying to kill you, you're defenseless, and no one will help. It could drive a person crazy. I later learned that the pulling on my legs was caused by a machine that is used to keep my blood circulating by tightening up every five minutes or so.

As the weeks lingered on I began to be

175

conscious much more often, but I was still severely delirious. At this point I still believed I was in England. I found it amazing that so many friends and family had traveled so far to see me, especially due to the fact that most of them did not have a lot of money. There was this janitor who always seemed to be in my room when I would wake up and I would tell him to get my tuxedo ready and to bring the car around, I have to get to the ball. I was in the middle of a very elaborate hallucination where I was some sort of 007 top secret spy agent on a mission. One day I woke up super pissed that my gear was not ready for the ball and my family was in the room. My sister came to my bed side "What ball? The Marine Ball?" she asked. "What in the hell is she talking about Marine Ball" I remember thinking. I could not even begin to imagine what my family was thinking by this point. I had been in ICU for a long time and for the longest time no doctor gave me a chance of surviving. Now that it seemed I was going to pull through and was waking up for a few minutes once a day or so, I seemed completely gone. I was loopy and no one had any idea what I was talking about. I'm certain that the doctors assured them that it was the morphine, but they knew I had a brain injury and I'm sure it was scary for them.

Finally I started waking up without hallucinating. There were high hopes for everybody. Sometimes I spoke normally, and sometimes I was a little off but I could hold a decent conversation. By this point I was moved out of ICU and now others besides family could visit me. Every day a doctor would come in and ask me a set of basic questions like what is your

176

name, ect. After a couple of weeks of this one day the doc asked me do you know where you are? Of course I knew where I was, England. "No, you are in Walter Reed Army Medical Center in Washington D.C. in the United States," the doc informed me. Now I was confused, but I started putting the pieces of information together and it made sense. After the doc left that day I asked my family why no one had told me that we weren't in England, since I knew I had brought it up several times. "We have been telling you every day for two weeks" my family argued back. This is the first time I really realized what bad shape I was in. Up to this point I was convinced that there were just some holes in my back.

One morning I woke up and there were people in my room, as always, chatting away. But something was different today. "Why are you whispering?" I inquired. Everyone was looking at me. I could see their lips moving, but I heard nothing. "What, What? I can't hear you!" I was growing frustrated. Why are they messing with me? This isn't funny! People kept trying to talk to me but I kept insisting that I couldn't hear. When the doctor came to see what was going on he assured my family that it was probably just the morphine playing tricks with my brain again. I went for a solid week day in and day out without hearing anything. One day my sister came in with a CD player and put the headset on me. I was still strapped down because sometimes I got the notion that I didn't want those tubes in me. My sister had gotten me the CD player with the knowledge of my love for music and the notion that it would pull me out of whatever trance I was in. She put the headphones on me, but I heard nothing. "Turn the volume up," I instructed. Still nothing, I insisted to her that it was broke. She put the headphones on herself, and they worked. I was completely and totally bilaterally deaf. The doctors began to run their tests. No one is sure to this day what caused the deafness. Could it have been the blast, the brain swelling, or even possibly the medication they gave me? Some lifesaving medications have neuro-toxins in them that can cause a person to go deaf. If this were the case I would be the lucky .01 percent. I think that this was the cause of my deafness. Why else could I hear all that time and then suddenly one day it just went away? I can't complain though. If I have to choose between deaf and dead I will choose deaf every time. As the months and years droned on and every doctor had to write to me and everyone became impressed with my attitude. For some reason I just never got down about it, it never really entered my mind that anything had changed. So what I couldn't hear I was still the same person.

I was finally beginning to stand, with help of course, and there were talks of starting rehab to help me learn how to walk again. I learned that I had taken a barrage of small arms fire to the back of the head causing a skull fracture and brain swelling, I also took 17 chunks of metal in the back. I had a breathing tube in my side for a long time because several rounds had punctured my left lung. I had a wet vac attached to me at all times for the first six months. I don't know, but to me that seems like a lot of blood. One day I was practicing baby steps in between the hallway wall with my physical therapist who was about 200lbs too light for the job, when a doctor approached me. "Weren't you just in ICU?" He asked. My physical therapist told him I was deaf, so he wrote it down. "Yes sir, but my room is right down here now," pointing the way. The doctor congratulated me on my miraculous recovery and told me that Someone had a plan for me. I went back to my room that day even more determined to complete a full recovery.

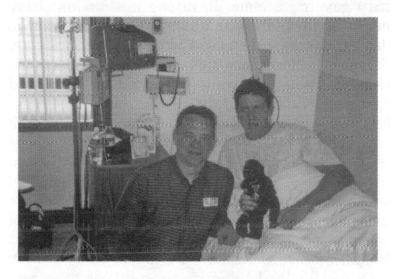

Honorary Ranger Tom Hanks making a visit to the Real Deal

One day a Ranger buddy of mine walked into my room. At first I couldn't help but think it was another hallucination, but I was excited to see him regardless. I asked him what he was doing here because he was with my group that was supposed to be still deployed. He informed me that he was shot a few days after me. I told him he looked awful good for a guy who just got shot and asked him where he was wounded. Keep in mind I had several family members in the room. This Ranger

179

proceeded to drop his pants and show me where several rounds had barely missed his manhood. Talk about lucky. My family all seemed embarrassed but the Ranger could care less. We talked for a few more minutes and then he was on his way.

By this time the rest of the Rangers had returned home and I had a few visitors from battalion. It was sure good to see them. One day one of the medics who had worked on me on the battlefield and Ranger Anderson paid me a visit. We were discussing which one of my nurses was the hottest when my lunch arrived. It looked disgusting of course. My Ranger buddies offered to go get me some good food from Wendy's which sounded like a great idea. But I had a better idea; I wanted to go with them. We got me rigged up in the wheel chair and told my nurse that we were just going to take a stroll around the hospital. When we reached the car we had to scrap the wheel chair. I will never forget the look on the cashiers face at Wendy's when I stepped up to order my Biggie sized meal. I had tubes coming from everywhere and I looked like I had escaped from a mental institution. I somehow survived that short trip but when my head landed on the pillow upon returning to my room I slept for a very long time. I simply was not ready for that much excitement.

Someone told the girl I had kind of been seeing in Savannah what happened to me and strangely enough, she was on the next flight to D.C. to see me. I didn't really want any girls to see me since I was still in pretty bad shape, i.e. I would still drool on myself from time to time. Nevertheless I was happy and shocked to see her. She stayed with me at the hospital for four days. One day the doctor came in and I couldn't think of any other way to introduce her than as my girlfriend. The doc looked at me very strangely but did not really question it. Sarah was getting ready to leave after spending what I felt were four pretty good days with me considering. Just before she left, she decided to break some bad news to me. "You won't see me when you get back to Savannah. I'm moving to Alaska." She wasn't kidding. What in the hell, she just spent four days with me and was all lovey dovey?! Girls!! You try to explain them!

The day after Sarah left, my doctor he asked "Tom what is going on?" I was confused. "What happened to your fiancé who came to visit you in ICU?" he asked. Now I was really confused. I told him I had no idea what he was talking about. I took me another week to find the answer. A childhood friend who lived in the area had come to see me, but since I was in ICU only family members were allowed to visit. Knowing this she bought a fake engagement ring and told them she was my fiancée. I told the doctor the funny story. He laughed, but I still don't think he believed me.

I had learned how to walk some with assistance, and the Army was getting ready to medivac me to the Tampa Traumatic Brain Injury Institute. I was excited. I was going to be close to home. Maybe they would even let me out for a weekend. But every day the time came to transfer me, something would happen and I would end up staying at WRAMC. During a MRI, the doctors found air in my head. Yes after all these years it was finally official, I was an airhead. They were afraid to put me on a plane because the pressure might make my head explode. Good enough reason for me. So I had to wait a few more weeks for the air to go away. During this time I was starting to get restless. Most of each day was spent in my room, with an hour at rehab, just to return to my room too tired do anything. Under no circumstances was I ever to try to walk out of my room alone. That didn't last long. I soon learned that there was a computer lab just down the hall from my room and I started making journeys there to email and whatnot. I got caught a few times and they threatened to strap me back down. Instead, they gave me my wheel chair back and told me I was only allowed to go to the computer lab and I always had to tell the nurse.

Finally the day came for my transfer. Two very high ranking personnel were escorting me which I didn't really understand. The whole time I was at WRAMC I also had a guard. A R.I. (Ranger Instructor...remember, from Ranger Training) that had been instructed to stay with me, he was an E-6. I was at WRAMC for a combined total of one year and met other Rangers who had been wounded. They always had some private or specialist as a POC (Point of Contact). I don't know why I was so special. On the flight to Tampa I asked the two Colonels why they were going to Tampa. They informed me just to drop me off and then they would head back to WRAMC. Not only that but I wasn't flying on your typical military plane but a private jet. It was very nice and made for a comfortable ride. When we landed, an ambulance came screaming onto the tarmac up to the plane. They quickly unloaded a stretcher and were waiting at the bottom of the stairs when I came walking off. Everyone was surprised; they were expecting something much worse. I got into the ambulance and they took me to the hospital, the wrong hospital. Good thing I wasn't in bad shape after all. On the way to the right hospital I made a deal with them that I wouldn't tell anyone of their error if they would get me Wendy's. Hell of a deal. I imagine it was a sight, an ambulance coming through the drive through with sirens flashing.

Back Home Back Home
Back Home Where I Belong.

So I was back in Florida, feeling better, and there was talk of possibly restoring my hearing. Everything was looking up. The first night that the nurses came in and changed my bandages one nurse gasped, "Oh my, what happened, were you in a car accident?" "No ma'am those are bullet wounds. I was shot in Afghanistan," I told her. They could hardly believe it. There were a few other military men there with terrible head wounds, but not nearly as many as I have. That first night in the Traumatic Brain Ward honestly scared me. The other Joes there with head wounds were much worse than I was. None of them were deaf, but you could definitely tell they had brain damage. One guy had taken a mortar round to the head. How in the hell do you survive that? He couldn't talk, walk, or do anything without help and he was always drooling on himself. When one nurse came to tuck me in that night she wrote to me, "Be glad that you can't hear. The guy in the next room over moans and screams all night." Wow, the first time I was glad to be deaf. But I found myself wondering, "Am I still in a delusion, am I really like all of these other guys but I just can't tell?" Scary!

As the weeks progressed with my rehabilitation, the doctors decided to let my family take me home for a weekend and we would see how I'd do. I was glad for a break from the hospital. I had rehab for one to two hours a day and then the rest of my day was spent twiddling my thumbs. The other guys in the ward who were able to converse would visit each other and spend the days talking. I was by far the youngest person in the entire place, so I guess I got blackballed, plus I'm sure no one wanted to write to me.

One day a beautiful young blonde around my age came in my room and informed me that she was the recreational therapist and I would be working with her for one hour a day over the next couple of weeks. Thank You Sweet Lord in Heaven. This became the highlight of my day. She didn't seem to mind sitting and writing with me at all. We would go bowling, go get ice cream which I didn't need as I was starting to pack on the pounds. Bowling was the funniest. I had become a pretty good bowler while in the Army because it's something cheap to do right on base. Things had changed though. I went from bowling around a 170 to bowling an 80, if I was lucky. I had to slowly approach the line and roll the ball with two hands down the aisle; it was like I was five years old again. My Ranger buddies would sure have a good laugh if they saw this. They would have a better laugh at me getting shot down day in and day out by this blonde.

After my wet vac came off and I was only receiving dry bandages twice daily, my rehab counselor decided we were going to shoot some hoops. I thought sweet, a chance to show off. Again my abilities let me down. In high school no one could touch me in basketball. I was the best. Today, I couldn't even hit the back board. Every time I would shoot the ball it was like the entire world would start shaking. If you have ever seen the movie *The Butterfly Effect* this is exactly what it was like.

My hair had grown very long over the months

and my beautiful blonde had promised she would take me to get it cut. On the way to the barber I couldn't resist any longer. "Am I retarded?" I asked. It seemed like a silly question even to me, but I honestly wasn't sure. Over the last few months I had experienced a lot of stuff and much of it wasn't true.

"No," she replied, "why would you ask that?"

"Well there are a lot of guys down my hallway that are in very bad shape. Sometimes it doesn't seem like they realize it at all," I told her. I continued "And to be honest, it used to be that no girl could resist my charm the way you have, I mean, who couldn't help but think it's because I'm retarded."

"No, no Tom that isn't it at all. You are a patient, I'm here to look after you not date you, that's all," she argued.

"Ok, I'm just saying cause there were a couple of nurses at WRAMC that didn't live by your creed I guess, whatever." I ended the argument. I know deep inside that she didn't like me because of what terrible shape I was in. Its ok, I bet she'd flip her lid if she saw where I am today.

Today was the day, I was going to be an outpatient, and was going to Gainesville. My best friend Carlos from Gainesville was coming to pick me up. I was going to try outpatient care and stay with Carlos who had so graciously agreed to change my bandages twice a day and drive me to the hospital daily. I would still have to go to the hospital every day, but at least I didn't have to sleep and eat there, and that raised my morale tremendously. I would be close to my friends and would have the weekends to myself.

After a couple of weeks of therapy at Gainesville VA, a group of my friends decided to float the river. It was a favorite pasttime amongst the group, me included. The river took about six hours to float and I was a little wary that I would not make it because I got tired easily still and slept most of the days away, plus I didn't want my wounds to get infected. My friends eventually talked me into it. At the entry point to the river I froze "Guys I don't think I can swim." Everyone laughed because everyone knew I could swim, but that was before being shot. Well you don't have to swim they assured me, you just have to float. At that point they helped me into the river and I will admit I was very shaky. Eventually I was situated on the float and we were moving along. It was a bit cool but the sun was shining nicely, and I was glad I came.

A little over halfway down the river my friends did what I was afraid they would do. They weren't trying to kill me; they just didn't know. Relaxing on my float I suddenly got that world is shaking feeling again. I was being flipped over. I went under water and immediately panicked, trying to resurface. I was swimming and swimming but not reaching the top. Carlos' hand scooped me up out of the water. I was gasping for breath.

"You assholes almost drowned me!" Everyone was laughing. They all thought I was kidding.

"Dude, we are shallow. You could have stood up at anytime very funny." Carlos stated.

"I'm serious I went under and it was kind of like I couldn't find my way up," I said with authentic fear. I guess they realized I was serious and apologized and agreed not to pull the stunt again. I made it home alive that day. Wouldn't that have been some shit to survive being shot 17 times only to drown to death under your best friend's hand a few months later.

The following Monday I told my therapist of the incident in full detail.

"Of course you couldn't find your way up. Your vestibular system has been destroyed. Swimming is the last thing you should be doing unsupervised," she informed me.

"Oh well, hey doc, thanks for telling me that ahead of time." I chimed in with sarcasm.

"Well most people don't try to swim a river before their wounds even completely heal," she made a good point. I couldn't help but chuckle at myself. "I tell you what. We have a pool therapist. I am going to set you up with her," the doc said. Oh God what have I got myself into now. I was growing very tired of the rehab. No matter how much I stood on that pillow and shook my head I just kept falling down. The rehab that I was currently going through consisted of "balance drills." Every day I would go to the hospital for hours on end and my doctor would have me stand on pillows, or try at least, and shake my head back and forth. That was the worst exercise. Some were better such as playing a simple game of catch to instill hand-eye coordination. To me it seemed I wasn't making any progress.

Pool Therapy day one. Thank You Sweet Lord in Heaven. My therapist was an absolutely gorgeous Latina named Vanessa, just a couple of years older than me. Therapy sucked because it was a heated pool for old people and I got overheated very easily. The first couple of weeks we just practiced walking in the water. She would try to get me to walk a straight line one foot in front of the other, which I never got right and always fell, conveniently into her so she would have to catch me. She loved how I made her laugh, I could tell. Soon we started swimming laps. They weren't hard laps at all but every time I was on the brink of passing out she would make fun of me.

Vanessa fought me for weeks with the same old story. "You're a patient and I'm your care provider. It's unethical." One day she broke. She knew that I had been taking sign language at the local community college at night, and one night I was leaving class when I spotted her. She tried to play it off that she was there for other reasons, but I saw through it. It was confirmed when I asked her if she wanted to get dinner with me since she was there anyway, and suddenly her plans had changed and she was free. We dated and had a blast the rest of my stint with the VA in Florida, but it was doomed to fail when I had to return to WRAMC so I guess I never really gave it a fair chance.

My wounds healed immensely while I was in Florida, but I didn't feel that my balance was improving very much. My most recent MRI had revealed that the swelling in my brain had reduced significantly and the doctors decided it was time for me to return to WRAMC to see about restoring my hearing, exciting!

WRAMC

I was told that I would only be in D.C. for no more than three weeks and then I must return to Savannah. I was told I didn't have a choice. It didn't matter to me. I would much rather be in Savannah than D.C. any day. Those three weeks turned into eight months of pure hell. I met with the doctors and audiologist, none of them were sure if I was a good candidate for the Cochlear Implant. The reason it is such a big decision is because the procedure and the equipment are extremely expensive and if it doesn't work, it is a waste. The day that my audiologist decided to go ahead with the procedure he still had no idea if it would work or not. The reason they were so unsure is that they still didn't know why I suddenly went deaf in the first place. The MRI's showed no damage to the nerve, so it should work, right?

The surgical procedure took place on December 21, 2004 and my "turn on" date was set for January 12. The reason for the gap in between is that after the procedure it takes time for the implant site to heal. Before the surgery I met with the anesthesiologist who went over the procedure with me.

"Any questions?" he asked.

"Well I guess just one, will this hurt?" acting like I didn't care.

"No, not at all, you won't feel a thing. When you come to we will keep you for a few hours to make sure that you're ok then you'll be on your way," he assured me.

When I woke up a few hours later in a hospital room rather than a recovery room and in dire pain,

I knew right away something had gone wrong. When the nurse saw that I was awake she came to me and handed me a note that said the surgeon would be coming to talk with me soon. Now I was certain something was wrong because he hadn't come to see me before the operation, so why come see me after? The nurse brought me some pain meds at my request, which is odd for me because I don't like to take medication. So I knew I was in serious pain.

When the surgeon arrived an hour or so later, his first question of course was, "How are you doing?" I replied very honestly. "Doc being shot didn't hurt this bad. What's wrong? The anesthesiologist told me that I wouldn't feel a thing, I'm damn sure feelin' something and it ain't good!" The surgeon chuckled slightly, "Of course it hurts. I just drilled a hole in your skull. Don't worry I got you some good pain meds coming to take with you and you get to wear this stylish cup on the side of your head for the next couple of weeks." I showed little interest in what the doc was saying. My mind was set on one thing.

"Hey doc can you send that anesthesiologist down here to see me? I want to talk with him?"

"No can do Ranger. I need him for an operation this afternoon. No roughing him up," Major McKinnon responded.

"Yeah well when you see him be sure to tell him I'm lookin' for him." I got in one last chuckle followed by a grimacing pain.

Twenty-four hours later they let me leave the hospital and go back to my hotel room. It was Christmas Eve, I was still in horrible pain, and alone. I didn't intend to get drunk sitting in the bar at the hotel that night, but as I sat there for hours I got very depressed. I was watching all of the other soldiers walking in and out. To my surprise I was the only one sitting at the bar. Every soldier had his own story. One would be on crutches, one wearing an eye patch, another in a wheelchair missing all of his limbs, and a deaf guy sitting at the bar feeling bad for himself drinking by himself on Christmas Eve. It just didn't seem right. Everyone of those soldiers I saw go by that night had a smile on his face. I thought, wow.

My girlfriend had arrived to spend Christmas Day with me which was a nice surprise. We decided to go to the Christmas Breakfast that a veterans group was hosting at the hotel that morning. As we exited the elevator I could see the festivities had already begun and everyone looked very happy. I just couldn't seem to understand or get happy myself, which is not the norm for me. Perhaps it was the medication I was taking.

We joined a friend I had made at WRAMC at his table with his mom. Jereme Coker had taken an RPG to the stomach and AK rounds in both legs on the convoy en route to the airport to bring him home for Thanksgiving. Today was Jereme's birthday! But not just any birthday, his 21st birthday. To be honest he looked like he was 16 years old, and when I first met him, I thought he was a cancer patient. Over the next few months as both of our injuries healed we became drinking buddies and began to escape the hospital and find our way around town to various bars.

Coker eagerly awaited the bar to open so that he could buy his first legal beer. At noon when the bar opened he was the first in line. He came swaggering back to the table where his mom, my girlfriend, and I were playing UNO and handed Katie and I a beer.

"Where's mine?" his mom piped up. Coker looked confused.

"You want a beer?...ok" As he was moving back to the bar in bewilderment his mom shouted, "What, how do you think you got here?" I roared with laughter. That was the funniest damn thing I had heard in my entire life. So my first Christmas home in the States in years was spent at Walter Reed Army Medical Center. But it wasn't so bad, I was surrounded by great people, heroes.

Ranger Wiggins and SPC Coker Visiting the WWII memorial in D.C.

The days kept inching toward that magical day when my hearing would miraculously return. I couldn't wait; I had become really frustrated by this point. I had dozens of notebooks slap full of conversations from the last year, but I always had faith that my hearing would "return". As I got closer to my Turn On Date, I started questioning what in the hell I would do if this contraption didn't work? I had kept a good spirit throughout the last year because I was so sure that I could be fixed, but I couldn't imagine being deaf for the rest of my life! What would I do for work? How would I live? Horrible thoughts crept into my head.

Finally January 12 arrived. I think I was visibly nervous as Dr. Schuchman led me to the testing room. He had as high of hopes as I did, but I could tell he was nervous too. He kept reminding me as he was setting up everything that it was going to be much different and that my hearing was not going to magically return, it would take some time before I would really start to perform well. No matter how many times he told me that, I still never fully comprehended it. It seemed to me like if this thing worked then wham, I could hear again, right? Dr. Schuchman hooked some wires to me and began the process, I eagerly waited...and waited...and waited.

The following is an article that ran in the *Army Times* about the procedure written by Michael E. Dukes, senior medical writer. I've included my personal thoughts in parentheses.

Doctor's at Walter Reed Army Medical Center performed a cochlear implant Dec. 12th to restore the hearing of a special operations Soldier who was wounded while serving in Afghanistan.

The implant is the first performed on a Soldier who was wounded while serving in the Global War on Terrorism, according to Dr. Gerald Schuchman, a speech pathologist with WRAMC's cochlear implant program. "To our knowledge, there hasn't been any other Army, combat related implant." (That's because most people die when they are shot in the head two times!)

Spec. Tom Wiggins, a Ranger from 1st Ranger Battalion of the 75th Ranger Regiment out of Hunter Army Airfield, Ga., was serving in Afghanistan when he was injured May 13, 2004 during a rocket propelled grenade explosion. After going through the medical evacuation process, he ended up at Walter Reed to be treated for closed head wounds, skull fractures, and neurological complications.

Wiggins, a 22-year-old Florida native, woke up one morning on Walter Reeds traumatic brain injury ward (actually the morning I woke up to silence I was residing in the Gyno Ward...try explaining that one to your Ranger buddies!) to absolute silence.

"It is extremely unusual to have absolute deafness," Schuchman said. "That's zero percent hearing," he explained.

Noting the effect on the Soldier, Schuchman said, "basic face-to-face communication was absolutely zero."

Wiggins carried a notebook everywhere he went. Wiggins and anyone he wanted to talk to used the notebook to write what they wanted to say.

In his nearly 35 years as a speech pathologist, Schuchman said he's never seen total deafness from a blast injury.

...Due to the extensive head injuries, there was a possibility that damage to Wiggins' cochlea wasn't the cause of his hearing loss – the problem could have been in the auditory nerve. Because of the root of Wiggins' hearing loss may have stemmed from his auditory nerve, doctors were uncertain if his hearing could be restored, but they

remained optimistic and decided to perform a cochlear implant.

...During the implant procedure, the eardrum is bypassed by making a small hole in the bone behind the patient's ear. A string of electrodes, thinner than a hair, is carefully fed into the cochlea.

The electrode array is attached to a microchip receiver/stimulator imbedded under the skin behind the patient's ear. It receives signals from an external minicomputer, or speech processor, which resembles a behind-the-ear hearing aid and stimulates nerves inside the cochlea with electrical signals to represent sound.

Three weeks after Mckinnon completed the procedure on Wiggins and the surgical site was healed, Schuchman met with Wiggins to turn on and test his new implant.

Schuchman placed the speech processor and coil portion of the implant behind Wiggins' ear and plugged a cable between it and a specially configured tuning laptop. Magnetically attracted to the receiver beneath Wiggins' skin, the coil looks like a black button stuck to his head. The magnetic connection stays firmly attached but the speech processor and coil can be removed with little effort.

After running through several sound settings on the implanted electrodes within Wiggins' cochlea, Schuchman began to get concerned...it appeared that the implant wasn't working in this patient. Refusing to give up, Schuchman continued with the testing. (This went on for over an hour; I could tell something was wrong. The doc and a lady from Nucleus would look at me and I would stare blankly at them, then I would get a fake smile and they would say they were still working on it, no problem. I was getting scared; I didn't really know what to do though.)

Finally, Wiggins' eyes snapped to Schuchman in an inquisitive way. "Did you ping me?" the Soldier asked. Immediately, a smile stretched across Schuchman's face; despite the odds, the implant had been a success. (Needless to say I was overwhelmed with happiness but I had a long ways to go and I didn't even realize it yet.)

"I was excited at first, but then I was a little frustrated," Wiggins said of his first day with the implant. But he said he reminded himself, "no, I have to be patient."

The sound cochlear implant patients hear is usually described as mechanical not melodic or smooth, often requiring months of therapy and practice to accurately comprehend...[END OF ARTICLE]

The following months were a new type of trial for me. I honestly believed that my hearing was magically going to come back once I had the cochlear implant; this is not the case at all. The average implant recipient takes about eighteen months to reach full potential and I was no different. I started off really well in that I could actually understand words the first day I was turned on; most people can not. I went through six months of speech therapy which wasn't so bad because my therapist was hot. I actually made it to all of my appointments; coincidence...I think not! The progress was SLOOOOWWWWW!!! I was getting to the point that I just wanted either to go back to my unit or be done with the Army altogether and it showed. I kind of stopped caring I guess you could say. Coker and I were drinking practically every day, and when he wouldn't go out with me, I would find someone else who

197

would. It was definitely a low point in my life.

One weekend Coker and I traveled out to Salisbury, a small town on the coast of Maryland. One of my childhood friends was living there and I was anxious for a change of pace. Matt is Josh's brother, who I joined the Army with. They also have a sister, Joanna, who had played the role of my fiancé when I was in ICU. They had come to visit me when I first came out of my coma and were, needless to say, shocked about how crazy I seemed to be. While they were visiting me, their father Dan Spencer passed away from a heart attack unexpectedly. Dan had been special to me as well as he had taken me into his home when I was 15 and let me live with them for free. So this night I had decided that for every shot we took, I would take an extra for Mr. Spencer. Before no time I was wasted! I don't really know what started it, but a ruckus broke out in the bar we were in and I somehow wound up getting involved. I think my frustration had been building up for months and this incident seemed to be my release. I picked up my bar stool and chunked it; this focused everyone's attention on me. Next thing I knew I was being rushed by four guys who didn't know what they were getting themselves into. I started kicking asses and taking names. Somewhere in the process my new hearing aid was knocked off my head and I realized it, so I started crawling around on the floor looking for it. Next thing I knew I was being picked up and pushed out the door by my buddies. As I opened the door I was greeted by a cop and he asked me, "How'd ya draw that blood?" pointing at my mouth. I just responded, "Guess someone got a lucky hit." I was instructed by the officer to sit on the sidewalk while he straightened the mess out. While I was sitting, a young lady came to me and returned my hearing aid. That was one sigh of relief. Then I saw the four guys who rushed me coming out the door all worked up telling their story to the cops. One of the guys started threatening me and I stood up and let him know anytime he was ready. About that time my buddy, Matt, came over to me and informed me that the four guys I had just busted up were off duty police officers. I was so drunk I just said, "Oh shit, guess they don't have a hand to hand training course to go through."

Well it looked like I was going to jail. As one officer put me in his cruiser, I muttered, "only in the north can you get arrested for a bar fight." As we were riding to the station for in processing, I asked my "chauffer" who all had been arrested. He told me I was the only person that anyone could identify. "Well this blood from my mouth didn't come from nowhere." I said sarcastically. I told him the other four guys had rushed me. He said, "Yeah, those guys are cops and they say that you started it." I knew that wasn't true because people were fighting already when I threw the bar stool. The young lady who returned my hearing said that she told the uniforms that I hadn't started it. She saw the whole thing.

It did no good. I sat in the slammer for a few days on $50,000 bond. FOR A BAR FIGHT! As it turned out, supposedly a couple of the off duty cops were hurt bad and one even had to have surgery. Finally my bail hearing came to order and several high ranking Special Forces guys and Coker were in attendance. MSG (Master Sergeant)

Thompson basically demanded that the judge release me into his custody. The judge complied!

As I approached the MSG coming from the jailhouse, I thought I'd try to take the edge off by cracking a joke. "Don't mess with me Sergeant. The inside made me hard!" To my surprise he laughed.

My trial was six weeks away, so I began calling in favors. I had met many political officials and big name lawyers while I was in D.C. who claimed if I ever needed anything to call them. I figured this classified. It sounded like a sham to everyone and we were all sure that I would walk with no problem; still I had some people make some phone calls. My fears were re-established when the DA refused to drop my charges. I had been charged with assault and reckless endangerment and here is the kicker. A lady got hit in the head with the bar stool and she is the town judges daughter and the sheriffs wife. It seemed I was up shit creek without a paddle.

I got a really good lawyer who offered to take my case for free. On my trial date I showed up at the shithole courthouse in shithole U.S.A. with one half of Special Forces with me. We were all decked out in Class A's. My lawyer and I were standing at the podium and the judge was talking to us. I had no idea what he was saying, I just kept shaking my head saying "yes sir." And then I guess he asked me if I was under the influence of any alcohol or drugs today. "Yes sir," I promptly replied. My lawyer immediately jerked his head in my direction. He then explained to the judge that I was deaf and could not hear. If I was so deaf why could I hear all of my buddies sitting behind me laughing their asses off?

My lawyer read off my resume to the judge who, I was assuming was ready to hang my ass, and then he asked to see the resume. After looking over it carefully he asked me if I had anything to say. Against my better judgment, I apologized for any wrong doings on my behalf. I was facing a max penalty of fifteen years imprisonment and an $8000 fine. I walked that day on a promise that I would never return to Salisbury, MD. Damn good deal as I never wanted to anyway. I paused for a sigh of relief. Here I was about to retire from the Army a "war hero," and if I had been convicted I could have been facing court marshal.

Finally, talk of my retirement started to be an everyday thing, and this excited me. I was ready to get back to Florida, though I had absolutely no idea what I was going to do when I got there. The hospital liaisons were having me attend practically every special event that they could just to keep me out of trouble; it was that obvious I did not want to be there anymore.

One of the events I was scheduled to attend was The Life Time Achievement Awards with a bunch of rich folks. That was all I was told, and that it would be open bar, but I was to behave because the Sergeant Major of the Army would be sitting at my table as well. Whatever, I didn't really care. At least I got Coker to go with me. The event was awesome though I couldn't really hear anything because it was so loud. Ed McMahon even came over to pay tribute to Coker and myself along with Tom Selleck and a few other celebrities.

On the way back to the hospital that night, Coker was telling me that Del Smith, who was our table host for the evening, had offered employment and to help with our schooling when we got out of the military. I wasn't interested in the slightest. I just wanted to get back to Florida with my friends, besides I couldn't go back to school in my current condition. Coker, however, was definitely excited about a chance to get out of Arkansas.

A week later, I was with Coker when he got a phone call informing us that we were to be outside the hospital in Class A's the following morning at 0800hrs. I was super pissed that I had to get up early and wanted to know why. Coker didn't have an answer for me. All he knew was that it had something to do with Mr. Smith who we had spent the evening with the week before.

At 0800 hrs a car picked us up and took us to a private airport where we met Mr. Smith and his stunning associate Blythe Berselli. There they informed us that we would be traveling with President Bush Sr. to his summer home in Maine. Coker and I snapped heads to look at one another. What in the hell?! Was this really happening? Why are we getting on a plane with Bush Sr.?

Sure enough, a few minutes later the ex-CIA Director and President's motorcade came screeching up to the plane. No one was searched, patted down, walked through a metal detector or anything. The President casually walked onto the plane and introduced himself. We spent the day in idle chit chat...WITH THE FORMER PRESIDENT OF THE UNITED STATES OF AMERICA! Coker and I shared our stories with the president and he seemed genuinely interested. He even asked us what all of our medals were...we knew that he knew what they were, but we indulged him anyway. It was one of the greatest events of my life up to that point and I will never forget it. More importantly Mr. Del Smith and Evergreen International now had my full attention.

Mainly to burn time, Coker and I got involved with the Horatio Alger Association, which had held the Life Time Achievement Awards, and got a $10M scholarship fund set up for returning veterans of the Afghanistan and Iraqi conflicts. It was during this time that I started to find my new passion for business. In general I enjoyed the atmosphere, the lunches, the meetings. While working on this project, I was able to meet many ambassadors and senators, including Bob Dole for the fifth or sixth time. I really like Dole because he comes to Walter Reed all the time to visit the troops.

A few weeks before my retirement, Coker was sent home to recoup there and rejoin his unit until the Army decided what they wanted to do with him. For me, the days seemed to drag on longer and longer. Finally the day arrived that I got to say goodbye to Walter Reed and the Army. I stopped through Savannah on the way home to say hi to the Rangers and inform them that I wouldn't be playing anymore as I was retired, AT 23 years of age!

I returned home to Gainesville, FL and everyone seemed happy to see me. I wasn't really doing anything and everyone else had jobs, so my time there didn't seem as grand as I thought it would be. I had kept in contact with Blythe from Evergreen (for more than one reason) and Coker and I had set up a week to go visit Oregon and check out Evergreen's corporate headquarters.

Coker and I spent a week checking out all of the Evergreen companies and local colleges. We were both 100% positive in no time that this was where we needed to be; the gods were smiling on us. I was really nervous about going back to school though, which was a part of the deal. I wasn't that good in school when I could hear, how would I do now?! I went home and packed my stuff and within two weeks I was moved to Oregon and ready to start school in the fall. Coker would still be a while trying to get out of the Army, so I would be absolutely alone on the West Coast for a while.

For about the first year I worked part time at several different Evergreen companies and went to school full time. Then in June 2006, Mr. Smith gave Coker and I another opportunity. He made us Co-Executive Directors of his world class Evergreen Aviation Museum Campus. In addition to this, we worked as ambassadors for Evergreen and have escorted such personalities as Bill O'Reilly, George Clooney, and of course we have also spent quite a bit of time with President Bush Sr. I have also been back to Afghanistan and Iraq numerous times with Evergreen. It does my heart good to see the difference we are making over there.

When I look back at the turns my life has taken over the last few years I find myself wondering: How is it that one day can change a person's life so much? And when was that one day? It may be cliché, but it's true. 9/11 affected every American citizen's life in one way or another, is this how it affected mine? Or perhaps it was the day I passed Ranger Training, or the day I was wounded.

Prior to 9/11 I was just a kid trying to get by,

not necessarily patriotic, and I definitely had never considered the military as an option. But it must have been hiding underneath there somewhere. We see it every time our nation calls for the strong; they arise. There are some people out there that always strive to be the best. When these people choose to join the military, they do become the best—they become Rangers. Being wounded rendered me deaf, but it has opened so many doors for me that I cannot believe. It also allows the world to plainly see how much I care for my country. While Americans are deeply grateful to their soldiers, they understand that they can never fully repay these warriors for their sacrifices. I know if I were in any other country my situation would surely be much different; I would probably be dead. From our medics training to our Veterans Affairs system no other nation in the world has given their soldiers care so much thought.

Although I am retired from the military I still constantly feel called. How can I help? How can I get back in the fight? That is why I continue to visit WRAMC, to offer wounded warriors the same opportunities that I received, to come work at Evergreen. They deserve a second chance. A lost leg, a lost arm, or even lost hearing is not a lost life. When a soldier is torn from duty he still carries a longing and passion to contribute to society and his country.

Currently I am a junior at one of Oregon's best colleges with a 3.8 GPA all while spanning the globe, managing a huge aviation campus, writing this book, and having the time of my life. I've learned that life is to short and nothing is promised so you can't wait for opportunities to arise, you must make them. It's been three years since my death and things couldn't be better. The moral of this story is...It ain't over till its over!